INDUSTRIAL LOCATION PLANNING

INDUSTRIAL LOCATION PLANNING

An empirical investigation of
company approaches to the problem
of locating new plants

by
STEN SÖDERMAN

ALMQVIST & WIKSELL INTERNATIONAL
Stockholm — Sweden

A Halsted Press Book
John Wiley & Sons
New York — London — Sydney — Toronto

First published in Sweden by
Almqvist & Wiksell International AB, Stockholm

ISBN 91-2200014-3

Published in the Western Hemisphere and the United Kingdom by
Halsted Press, a Division of John Wiley & Sons, Inc., New York

Library Congress Catalog Card No.: 75-6286
Halsted Press ISBN 0 470-81045−9

Soc
HD
58
S58

Printed in Sweden by
Göteborgs Offsettryckeri AB, Stockholm 1975

CONTENTS

PREFACE

In a book review recently I read about Faludi´s book Planning Theory, published in 1973. The reviewer calls the author the last of the rational planners and says that "planning theory in the Western democracies has taken a new turn in which rational and non-rational elements are viewed as inevitably mixed in what is coming to be known as the new humanist style of planning". [1] I dare say I share this opinion. The importance of non-rational elements when constructing theories has become more and more obvious to me during the course of the study.

When I launched this project some years ago, however, one of my basic starting-points was a number of models of an operational analysis character. As a matter of fact, my research question at that time was: "How should companies behave in situations of location choice?" The approach adopted aimed at formulating procedures for reaching optimal company solutions. After formulating a normative model, I tried to collect data with the idea of proving its applicability. In 1971, the approach taken by three Swedish companies to the problem of locating new plants was studied. This attempt was frustrating. The assumptions of the model were supported only to a very limited extent.

A search for more reasonable assumptions about company behaviour was then initiated. This was done, primarily through the study of literature describing actual cases of location behaviour. This contributed little to my knowledge, and the persistent lack of reasonable assumptions made the construction of a normative model practically impossible. Consequently, I had to question my original aim. My conviction grew stronger that it was more important to understand real decision-making processes than to construct normative models. This phase of my research took place within the Department of Business Administration at Stockholm University.

During my academic year (1972/1973) at Queen´s College, Oxford University. I further concentrated on studies of actual company behaviour in situations of industrial location planning. In order to broaden my empirical base, I gathered information on location planning in two British companies. This made me finally drop the normative ambitions and instead engage myself in a purely descriptive investigation. The following research question was now formulated: "How do companies behave in situations of location choice, i.e. when they face the problems

---

1/ Regional Studies, Numbers 3/4, November 1974, p. 311

of when, how and, primarily, where a location or a branch location should be made?" During my stay in Oxford I obtained a scholarship enabling me to receive advice from the European Institute for Advanced Studies in Management (EIASM) in Brussels.

My continued work at the Department of Business Administration in Stockholm was a combination of literature study and empirical investigation, leading to the construction of a basic model, later elaborated in my so called extended model. This model expressed my conception of company behaviour in an industrial location choice situation and the final field study of 25 cases based on interviews was made in the spring and summer of 1974. My work on this thesis has thus been carried out in a number of different settings.

Although I later changed the original aim of my research which had been inspired by Göran Bergendahl, he continued to show great interest in the progress of my study. Lars Persson has also greatly encouraged my work. His willingness to take part in discussions and, in particular, his immediate reactions on all my drafts have been of great value. He has had a strong influence on the entire study and has contributed largely to this final version.

Other researchers with whom I have had the pleasure of exchanging ideas and who have affected my work are Jay Galbraith, Donald Hay, Anthony Hopwood and participants in seminars held at the Department of Business Administration at Stockholm University and at EIASM in Brussels. I am also grateful to many others for their assistance in my work. The following list is by no means exhaustive: Igor H Ansoff, Carl-Johan Bouveng, Björn Leonardz, Jens Lindberg, Bo W:son Schyberger, John Skår, Agneta Söderman and Solveig Wikström have read all or main parts of my drafts and their suggestions are reflected in the present version. Agneta Frösslund, Bengt Kjellén and Lars Rudefors wrote protocols from the main parts of the interviews and they have also assisted in the preparation of the final manuscript.

Rickard Schéle helped with the statistical computations. Nancy Adler and Pat Mitchell transformed my manuscript into correct and clear English. Astrid Normann drew the figures, Eva Åhrell made the cover and Inga-Britt Aggeklint assisted in checking the references. I have also had the advantage of an excellent secreterial service provided by SIAR´s (Scandinavian Institutes for Administrative Research) Stockholm office. Immense and loyal efforts to transform my hand-writing into a readable book have been devoted by Birgitta Eriksson, Kerstin Håkansson, Gunilla Höijer, Eva Jonson and Birgit Östin.

Finally, I want to thank all the company executives who kindly permitted me to take their precious time for long and exhaustive interviews.

Financial support for this research project has mainly been given by the Swedish Council for Social Science Research and the Stockholm University.

Stockholm, April 1975

Sten Söderman

"Hallo!" said Piglet, "what are you doing?"
"Hunting," said Pooh.
"Hunting what?"
"Tracking something," said Winnie-the-Pooh very mysteriously.
"Tracking what?" said Piglet, coming closer.
"That´s just what I ask myself. I ask myself, What?"
(Winnie-the-Pooh)

CHAPTER 1   SOME STARTING-POINTS

The regional problem from the government point of view is briefly presented. Prior research from the field of location problems is then described by introducing successive limitations. This serves to define the research problem and also reveals some aspects of my approach. The chapter concludes by posing five research questions which will be answered in the subsequent six chapters.

1.1 The Regional Problem

Although the aim of this study is to contribute to the knowledge and understanding of the behaviour of the individual company when making location decisions, it seems reasonable to start with a description of the wider context in which such decisions are made.

Usually the concept of industrial location is associated with regional problems and policy i.e. means and ends on a national level. The regional problem is a natural component of economic development. A rising standard of living brings about changes in industrial structures and patterns of trade, all of which tend to favour some regions and penalize others. These changes have always taken place, but have been particularly marked since the industrial revolution fundamentally altered the economic structure of the more advanced countries.

1

However, the idea that these forces could or should be controlled by Government policy is very recent. The origins of Swedish regional policy may be traced to the 1950's and for most European countries regional policy is a post-war creation; the exception being Britain whose policies originate in the late 1920's (Brown, 1972, p. 281). Nearly all Western European nations now apply measures which may be properly described as regional policy (McCrone, 1969, p. 13) though the nature of the regional problem differs from country to country. A few examples will illustrate this. In the United Kingdom the very high population density, implying a highly urbanized society, has led to special problems. Furthermore the historical factors also play a part as Britain was the first nation to industrialize. The regional problem in Britain is therefore predominantly one of depressed industrial areas such as the North-East of England and South Wales.

There also exist in Britain areas of rural depopulation and underdevelopment, the best known examples being the Scottish Highlands and Mid-Wales (ibid, pp. 16-17). Regions with similar characteristics can be found in the northern parts of Scandinavia and Finland and also in the mountain areas of Austria and Switzerland (EFTA, 1971, p. 16).

In most countries regional development policies have come about in response to a mixture of political, social and economic pressures and it is not always possible to say which has played the dominant role. The existence of regional unemployment on a serious scale seems to be the factor which exerts the greatest influence in inducing Governments to take action. But this action is probably prompted as much by the political consequences of unemployment and the social need to give everyone an opportunity to work as it is by the desire to make the best use of the nation's economic resources. It is therefore insufficient to consider a regional development policy as if it were purely an economic decision (McCrone, 1969, p. 25).

In Sweden, as in most other developed countries, there has been an increasing migration of people and of companies. The causes and effects of this process and the important changes of structure and urbanization have been studied over a period of years. Some public reports have examined the means and ends of the regional policy and also to some extent the motives of the firm. These studies (see e.g. SOU 1951:6, 1963:49 and 1969:49) have influenced the Swedish Parliament to implement various instruments for control, such as location grants and loans. During the autumn of 1974 another public report was published, SOU 1974:82 "Samverkan för regional utveckling" in which a new government authority "Statens lokaliseringsdelegation" is proposed. This organization would coordinate all location activities and grant permission to the majority of locations. This is more restrictive than earlier instruments of government control and its primary purpose is to reduce unemployment in different regions.

Although concern for the spatial distribution and movement of manufacturing industry has thus been an important feature of public policy for more than twenty years in Sweden, the flow of relevant theoretical and empirical work has been relatively low until eight or nine years ago. Much of the work was coordinated by ERU (expertgruppen för regional utredningsverksamhet) a government research group which was set up (in 1965) to initiate and coordinate regional research in Sweden. Original research on regional and location problems has also recently been carried out at the Stockholm School of Economics and at Umeå University. Some of these studies, which relate directly to this research, will be referred to later on. However, though attempts have been made to construct a theory of location based on the canons of neoclassical economic price theory, these attempts have not generally been very satisfactory in terms of explaining empirical results or in predicting changes in the patterns of corporate relocation (Townroe, 1971, p. 2). It is possible that insufficient effort has been devoted to investigating the location choice process of the individual firm.

1.2   The Problem to be Studied

There is an alternative to looking at plant location in the context of regional planning, and that is to examine it from the viewpoint of the individual firm. Looked at in this way it becomes a process of selecting, from amongst a variety of sites, the best on which to establish a new plant. Government incentives are clearly only one of a number of factors affecting this process.

Whereas the preceding section concerns the ultimate effect of location decisions on society, this second view is concentrated on the decision-making process within the firm.

This study will examine location problems from the second viewpoint – that is from the perspective of the firm and the individuals within it who are involved in the selection process. More precisely the question to be answered is: How do companies behave in situations of location choice, i.e. when they face the problems of when, how and, primarily, where a relocation or a branch location should be made?

An important clarification of the subsequent treatment concerns the "physical object". This study treats site selections of industrial plants which manufacture goods. It therefore only considers problems that are generally included in the concepts of "plant location" or "industrial

3

location". Problems of "retail location" or "warehouse location" are excluded. The former, in which factors of demand are of dominant importance, are dealt with in, for example, Applebaum (1965) and Borin (1967). The latter, in which transportation costs predominate, are discussed by amongst others, Kuehn & Hamburger (1963).

In addition this study does not deal with the location of offices. Research about this type of location problem has been aimed at the construction of patterns of information flows and systems of contacts. In England the relocation of offices out of the London area, and in Sweden the relocation of offices and of certain government authorities, have been studied and are documented in for example Bateman, Burtenshaw and Hall (1971), SOU 1970:29 and Thorngren (1972).

From now on the concept of location will have two meanings: (1) the act or process of localizing conducted by individual actors in the company and (2) the geographical position. In those cases where it is important to clarify the exact meaning, the word "localization" will be used to denote the process and words such as "site" and "position" to denote the geographical position.

Finally the generality of the localization process must be commented upon. Despite the differences in the regional problems of different countries, the nature of the localization problem from the company´s viewpoint is assumed to be the same in principle. This assumption is based on evidence from the study made by EFTA (1971, pp. 36–49) covering eight European countries and from the bulk of references that are presented on the pages which follow.

1.3   The Need for Studies on Location Problems

There is little mention in the literature of the role played by government incentives and subsidies. The need for increased knowledge is therefore apparent so that the efficiency of this instrument of government control may be determined. It is particularly important to understand the forces governing location choice before further control instruments are established.

The following figures express one measure of public policy: during the period 1.7.1965 – 30.6.1973 a total of 2,225 million Skr was spent and 30,989 extra jobs provided to stimulate regional economic activity (AMS. Meddelanden från utredningsenheten, 1973:20). The need for this knowledge is very apparent when one studies the most recent public report on location in Sweden (SOU 1974:82). No attempt is made in this document to understand the process which takes place within a company before the final site selection is made. Briefly, the report argues that although existing instruments of government control are utilized in an optimal way, the goals of regional policy will not be reached without introducing "compulsory location control".

An entrepreneur´s choice of location for his firm is probably one of the most important decisions he will ever make. It fixes the location from which he is henceforth obliged to purchase his raw materials, his semi-finished products and his energy. It establishes the size and quality of the workforce available to him and, in some cases, it defines the markets in which he can sell his products. What is more, once the decision is implemented there can be no turning back. The financial implications of moving a second time will, in almost all cases, force him to stay where he is.

Knowledge about location processes would therefore also be useful to the individual firm. It has been proved that the profitability and/or productivity of a plant is dependent on its geographical location. The wage differences within Sweden can reach 20 % according to a study by Jobin (1973, p. 12) and according to another piece of empirical research the regional differences in productivity, when comparing sites in the Stockholm area and some other regions, were up to 20 % (Åberg, 1973, p. 141). The "advantages of communication" are unevenly distributed between regions with different population densities. In a recent investigation it is argued that passenger air communication with the rest of Sweden is twice as good from the Stockholm region as from the forest counties (skogslänen) (Törnqvist, 1972).

The last though by no means the least significant argument for understanding the location problem is that present location models, using traditional location factors (see section 1.6), are quite inadequate. This argument is naturally closely linked to the fact that little attention has been paid to matters such as the limited information upon which a choice of location is often based (Townroe, 1971, p. 15). In addition the development of some understanding of the types of criteria employed and the methods by which alternatives are generated and evaluated could also give valuable insights into the ways used to solve a variety of ill-structured problems.

1.4 Choice Theories and Process Theories on Location Problems

The problem of location, seen from both the government´s and the company´s point of view, has been studied from the perspective of a number of different disciplines. With some exceptions it can be said that economists have determined optimal patterns of location, geographers have studied existing spatial patterns and disciples of operations research have examined the choice between alternatives in well-structured situations where the criteria are well defined.

In the course of the years when theories of location problems have
evolved they have naturally focused on different aspects of the decision
itself and the process by which it is reached. These theories can
therefore be classified according to one or more dimensions with
extreme points such as descriptive/normative and satisfying/optimizing.
Although this may help provide a rough description of a particular
theory it is often too crude. Hopefully a theory will some day emerge
that cuts across these dichotomies. In this study I shall adapt a
classification in terms of choice theories and process theories from
MacCrimmon (1970). Choice theories are concerned with the choice
itself and procedures for reaching optimal solutions, whereas process
theories focus on the process that precedes the choice, with the solution being some satisfactory by-product of the decision process. One
may say that, in general, choice theories are normative whereas
process theories are descriptive.

The choice theories are mainly based on economic theories of equilibrium including a number of assumptions, such as perfect competition.
Historically this approach has dominated the theories of location
problems and this has been the basis of the neoclassical location
theories presented by Weber (1909), Lösch (1954), Isard (1956) and
Greenhut (1956). Some other examples of location studies also including conditions of equilibrium are found in Lefeber (1958), Guteland
(1968) and Serck-Hanssen (1970).

In these theories of location the equilibrium condition assumed that
each company was optimally located. Thus equilibrium was reached
by a long series of individual moves in which each actor behaved ration-
ally to optimize his circumstances.

The recent development of operations research models is often based
on and can be seen as an extension of this neoclassical tradition with
heavy reliance on the transport factor. The orientation towards the
development of algorithms is always based on well-structured problem
situations. In Nieckels & Söderquist (1970) and Revelle, Marks and
Liebman (1970) surveys of some of these problem formulations, models
and algorithms are presented. Since the purpose of this study is descriptive rather than normative the choice theories are of little use here.

However the process theories which are based on the observed factual
behaviour of the companies relate directly to this research. Three
groups of studies are here identified.

I. The selection of a site for an industrial plant can be, but has not
often been, regarded as a special case of the selection between capital
investment projects. These decisions and the preceding processes

have been studied by a large number of authors. Among these studies I particularly stress Aharoni (1966), who treats foreign investments, and Bower (1970), who describes four planning processes in a large divisionalized company. Finally Junnelius (1974) examines the capital budgeting process in different types of organization structures.

II. Some theories behind general decision-making constitute an important frame of reference for this study. These theories shall be described in section 1.5.

III. Theories or rather fragments of theories and existing empirical observations primarily oriented towards localization processes and subsequent decisions will be further presented below in section 1.6.

1.5   Theories on General Decision-Making

The empirical literature in this vast research field neatly divides into three groups: <u>individual decision-making</u> - largely studied in game situations by cognitive psychologists; <u>group decision-making</u> - primarily researched through laboratory methods by social psychologists; and <u>organizational decision-making</u> - researched in the field of organizational and political theory.

The research on <u>individual decision-making</u>, perhaps best represented in the book by Newell & Simon (1972), largely relies on eliciting the protocols of decision-makers as they try to solve simplified made-up problems. These protocols are analyzed in order to develop computer simulations (e.g. GPS) of the decision processes apparently being used. Although there is a great jump from the simulation of a chess move (one type of problem under study) to the location of a plant, the research does, nevertheless, provide some general conclusions which relate to the study of location decision processes.

Specifically, studies of individual decision-making have found that, faced with a complex, unprogrammed situation, the decision-maker is very constrained by his own cognitive abilities. As a result, he seeks to simplify his situation - to split the big decision into sub-decisions, and to reduce these into elements sufficiently simplified so that he can apply general, interchangeable sets of procedures which are familiar to him. Hence, the decision-maker deals with unstructured issues by changing them into familiar, structurable elements. Furthermore, the individual decision-maker uses a number of problem solving habits - seeking solutions that are satisfactory instead of optimal, not looking too far ahead, reducing a complex environment to a series of simplified conceptual models.

7

Hence, we can conclude that although the processes used are not explicit and predetermined there is some evidence that a basic rationale or structure underlies the behaviour of the decision-maker, and this structure can be described by a systematic study of his behaviour.

The research into group decision-making, carried out primarily in the social psychology laboratory, is extensive, but much of it is concerned, not with the structure of the decision process, but with the interactions among the participants. As will be evident throughout this study, the structure of the location decision processes is above all determined by their complexity; over-simplification of such processes in the laboratory removes the very element on which this research should be focused.

The research on organizational decision-making is extensive. However it must be pointed out that much of the literature on decision-making, policy formulation and planning concerns attempts to formalize rational policy making i.e. "to lay out explicitly the necessary steps in the process" (Lindblom, 1959, p. 80). Since my approach is descriptive such literature is of little use in this study.

The early study of a business decision (the use of EDP equipment) by Cyert, Simon and Trow (1956) at Carnegie Mellon University is of special interest as are a number of subsequent studies stimulated by it. Cyert & March (1963) reported on four decision processes; two in fact were further analyses of sub-decisions of the early study (selection of a consulting firm and choice of a data processing system), while two were new studies (accelerated renovation of old equipment and search for new quarters for a department). Since their "behavioural theory" deals with general decision-making in a "large multiproduct firm" and I consider location decision-making in firms of any size and of any number of products I do not intend to base my study explicitly on the concepts of this well-known theory. Lindblom (1959) presents two methods: "Rational-Comprehensive (Root) and Successive Limited Comparisons (Branch)". The "Rational" method was dismissed above. Lindblom also argues for the second method which he calls "muddling through", when analyzing complex problems. Since location processes are complex, this second view may relate to this study. Finally the research by Cohen, March and Olsen (1972) which is in line with the Lindblom ideas may be referred to. The authors here present a model for a garbage can decision process.

1.6 Theories and Empirical Observations on Localization Processes

I have decided to group the research on localization processes and decisions under three main headings.

1. Traditionally the empirical research on location decisions has used the location factor approach. As has already been indicated the various location factors, such as market, transport and raw materials, hold a position of primary importance in the general literature of location. In these studies the same principal question is asked: "Why was this site selected? Rank the factors that influenced you in the selection of this site on the list presented!" Three approaches seem most frequent.

First the general approach, which is not linked to any region or specific industry. Secondly an approach which is based on plant locations in a specific "area". The question often asked in this case is: "Why did you select this region?" A third approach is to draw the sample from a specific industry.

In the table below a sample of existing location factor studies is presented.

"general":	Katona & Morgan (1952), Törnqvist (1963) (=SOU 1963:49), Morgan (1967), Carrier & Schriver (1968), Fulton (1955, 1971)
"area":	Greenhut (1959), Mueller, Wilken and Wood (1961), Hunker & Wright (1963), McMillan (1965), Stevens, Brackett and Coughlin (1967), Kruse (1972)
"industry":	Dikeman (1962)

There are, however, some weak points in the location factor approach as far as this study is concerned. First, the factors to be ranked have been identified by the researcher and not by the respondent. Secondly, it is normally only possible to reach the triggering location factor or factors. Knowledge about the process of steps taken inside and outside the firm that has led to the existing position is therefore small or nonexistent. Thirdly, these empirical studies, using survey methods (interview or mail questionnaire) as a tool of investigation, are based on the assumption that the original reasons for making a location decision are identical with the opinion of a particular representative of the firm who is not always the key actor in the site selection process.

Note: The term "factor", together with the term "variable", will be frequently used throughout the study. A precise definition of these terms can be found in section 3.1.

2. The models and theories on industrial location processes are far from extensive. However in the following six studies, which all relate directly to this research, stepwise procedures or models are presented. In five of them: Hamilton (1968, p. 365), Townroe (1969, p. 20), Krumme (1969, p. 37), Lloyd & Dicken (1972, p. 147) and Rees (1972, p. 203) the steps are formulated in figures while in the sixth study by Stafford (1969) there is a verbal presentation. All of these share with my own study a common basis in adaptations of Simon's (1945) subjectively rational decision model including uncertainty and sub-optimal behaviour. The most significant common features are: problem recognition, search, evaluation and final decision.

Only two of the six models (the studies by Rees and Townroe) are based on location processes actually investigated by the authors. The Rees model was modified (this is the expression used in Rees, 1972, p. 203), after open-ended interviews had been conducted with recent location decision-makers in large American corporations setting up new branch plants. It is not completely clear what degree of support the Townroe model received. However the most promising publications in this field for the purpose of this study are published by Townroe. His pioneering work is presented in a book (1971) and in two articles (1969 and 1972) and concerns one empirical investigation in England.

Townroe interviewed 59 firms, 45 outside and 14 inside a Development Area, about the pressures which produced the decision to move, the search for a new site, the evaluation of alternatives and the final choice (1971). A further analysis of the same data where the behaviour is related to the "structure of the company", the "type of move" and to the "usual factors of push and pull" was conducted in Townroe (1972). Chi-square tests were used to search for interrelationships and a principal component analysis was applied to yield characteristic groups of companies. The result showed great heterogenity of behaviour and a wide divergence from an a priori pattern of "good management". Despite this, however, the article concludes with a number of "general hypotheses".

3. The third group contains case descriptions of real localization processes. I have found four principal collections of such case-studies: Neuhoff (1956) - 7 cases; Luttrell (1962) - 98 cases; Whitman & Schmidt (1966) - 1 case; and Townroe (1971) - 6 cases. After short descriptions of these studies some general conclusions will be drawn.

In Neuhoff (1956) the "prevailing practice", i.e. a stepwise decision procedure is presented. The steps concern:

- Organization: centralized staff group, decentralized function, committee, company and operation. - New plant requirements. - Selection of general area. - Screening communities: sources of information, use of company name. - Final comparison. - Selecting a site.

Seven case-studies are then described in a systematic way. All of them show minor variations in the procedure above. Nothing is said about uncertainty but the different steps taken by these rather large American companies are very rational.

Luttrell´s book "Factory location and industrial movement" (1962) is the most comprehensive research published in the field. This is a British study on the problems of setting up manufacturing plants on new sites, particularly branch factories in the Development Areas and elsewhere. It is based on 98 case-studies of plants set up during the period 1945-1952. The aim is to compare costs of operation between the new branch and the parent factory, for each of the branch´s early years. The aim is also to examine other aspects and circumstances including the selection of the site, the recruitment and training of workers, the transfer of key people, communications and transport, changes in manufacturing technique and the size of operations.

In March 1962 the big American company, General Foods Corporation, announced that its board of directors had authorized funds for site selection and preliminary engineering for a new food processing plant to be located within 250 miles of New York City. The new facility - part of the company´s Jell-O Division - would replace four older plants located in the northeastern part of the United States and would consolidate all their various operations under one roof. This case history is carefully described by Whitman & Schmidt in the book "Plant relocation" (1966). The performance after the move is also described.

In his book "Industrial location decisions" (1971) Townroe briefly describes six of the 59 cases which he investigated. The descriptions contain some stepwise indications of the site selection procedure but nothing on the performance after the move.

In addition some Swedish research (Stockholm School of Economics) should be mentioned. One study was reported by Back, Dahlborg and Otterbeck (1970). After interviewing 40 managing directors the authors conclude that a location problem cannot be characterized by one or a few location factors of the usual type. A location problem cannot be treated simply as a minimizing of the transport cost with some restrictions. "A location must be seen as a process, where many factors co-operate" (ibid., p. 301). For confidential reasons the presentation

of the findings is divided into a number of types of location factors instead of describing each case. This makes it difficult to use this study
as a source of conclusions. In a study by Otterbeck (1973) a small
number of cases are briefly described in a manner similar to Townroe.

Although some of the case-studies included in the literature seem to be
based on rationalizations, some conclusions about the features of the
location selection situations can be made.

The location decision is <u>only one of the array of decisions</u> that a firm
has to make in order to adapt to alterations within the firm or its environment. The geographical variable thus strongly depends on, and at
the same time influences, other decision variables such as the choice of
product, product mix, the increase or decrease in capacity and the
selection of manufacturing process.

Another feature is the lack of experience of location decision -making in
a firm. Since a location decision is made very rarely, perhaps only
once in a lifetime, the lack of relevant experience greatly affects the
type and quality of the decision made. Of course location problems are
sometimes approached in a systematic and routine manner, especially
when carried out by bigger firms. However, in general we would anti-
cipate that both the quantity and quality of the location planning process,
would be affected first by the planner's previous experience and secondly by his expectations of having to do similar work in the future. The
location problem is therefore often <u>low programmed</u> or <u>non-routinized</u>.
(See March & Simon, 1958, p. 143 on the concept of programming.)

The lack of programming is also caused by the nature of the location
problem itself. This is generally complicated by the large number of
important factors involved and the complex relationships between these
factors. In some situations the choice is between competing alternatives but in many others it is one of the acceptance or rejection of a
single course of action. The criteria are not the same from one choice
to another; one choice may be made on the basis of relative costs and
savings while the next may be based entirely on qualitative criteria.
Furthermore few, if any, locational choices are based on a single criterion. This kind of problem, when neither the criteria for accepting
a solution nor the data upon which it is based are particularly well
defined, are said to be ill-structured. (See Newell, 1969, p. 404 on
the concept of ill-structured problems.)

It is furthermore difficult to <u>validate</u> the location process and the
succeeding choice since a location decision which afterwards seems to
be a "good" decision might have been preceded by a "bad" procedure
through which the worst alternative from a set of very "good" alterna-

tives was chosen. On the other hand one must regard it as a "bad" decision if a carefully conducted procedure results in the choice of the "best" of a set of "bad" alternatives.

1.7   Classification of Localization Situations

Having presented the theoretical and empirical frames of reference some concepts will be defined before the precise research questions are formulated.

First, neither "relocation" nor "branch location" have been given precise definitions. Unfortunately there are no generally accepted definitions – nominal or operational – of these terms in research studies published in Sweden. The criteria used by a number (9) of different authors to define establishments, relocations and branch locations vary. The total number of criteria for nominal definitions is eight and no two authors use the same combination of criteria. This is shown in an accurate study by Levin (1974).

Lacking a commonly accepted definition I must therefore introduce my own which are as follows:

"Relocation" means that a company has closed down an existing factory and moved its manufacturing facilities to a new factory.

"Branch location" means that a company has built a new factory which will function in addition to its existing factory or factories.

Since this study is of a descriptive character it is necessary to make quite clear what will be meant by a "localization situation" and what kinds of situations these are. Some further classifications will therefore be presented to delimit and define the concept of location.

1. Two principal kinds of location processes can be identified: those which lead to a final decision and those which are interrupted for some reason before any kind of final answer is produced. Though these interrupted decisions would be interesting to examine, only those location processes which are completed will be considered in this study.

2. Initiated location processes that have led to final decisions can be sub-divided as well. On the one hand there are decisions which result in the company´s remaining on its existing site, and on the other there are those which result in the establishment on a new site.

13

Data illustrating the frequency of these three practical situations
are rare. Concerning the first classification I have found nothing.
Concerning the second, if we divide industrial location decisions
into "old-site" and "new-site" then the former predominate. Globally
sixty to eighty per cent of new manufacturing capacity each year is
allocated to the expansion of existing plants according to a report
for the United Nations (1967, p. 17). These two methods of classification are illustrated in the decision tree below. Only the branch
to the extreme left is considered in this study.

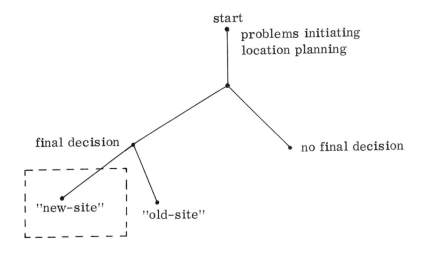

3. A common classification ascribed to Hoover (1948, p. 36) is this:
    There are three kinds of locations as far as the degree of "foot-
    looseness" is concerned. For effective production some industries
    are "tied to" areas of specific raw material supply, some to speci-
    fic markets and some, finally, are called "footloose". Only the
    category which is free to locate "anywhere" will be considered
    here. Luttrell estimated that about two-thirds of British industry
    could be considered "footloose" (1962).

4. The term "new-site" can be further sub-divided. Since the aim is
    to study activities within the company in which participants are en-
    gaged, an attempt will be made to isolate these activities as much
    as possible. There are two basic decisions which must be made
    before the search is started. First, should the search be for a
    bare site or for a site with a building on it? And secondly should
    the building be an empty factory or a functioning plant with an
    established workforce? Both bare sites and those with a factory
    already on them will be considered in this study. However the
    situation in which the new factory has an established workforce

14

introduces factors which relate to "mergers" or "takeovers", rather than the central issue of site selection. The study will therefore only consider situations where a "new" workforce is required.

To sum up, I have made the following definitions and restrictions:

1. Only processes that have led to a final decision will be studied. This implies a retrospective approach.

2. The location must be on a "new" site.

3. Only footloose industries are considered.

4. It is unimportant whether the site has a building on it or not.

5. The workforce must be "new".

This can also be illustrated in the figure below:

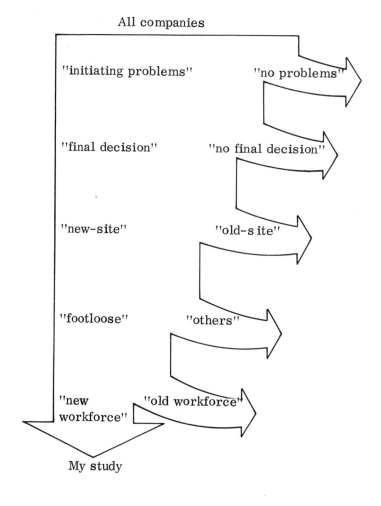

All companies

"initiating problems"   "no problems"

"final decision"   "no final decision"

"new-site"   "old-s ite"

"footloose"   "others"

"new workforce"   "old workforce"

My study

1.8   The Research Questions

The basic question of this study is: "How do companies behave in situations of location choice, i.e. when they face the problems of when, how and, primarily, where a relocation or a branch location should be made?" The manner in which this question should be answered is dictated by the discussion in the preceding sections which proves the importance of describing actual localization processes and indicates the need for field observations. With this essential conclusion in mind, an answer to the basic question will be sought by posing and answering the five further questions shown below.

1.   What forces - variables and factors - affect the behaviour in location choice situations, i.e. in localization processes?

2.   What are the general variables and factors and how are they related?

3.   How should a field study be designed to verify the generality of the variables, factors and relationships?

4.   How can the data from the field study be described and interpreted?

5.   In view of the findings, what implications and improvements can be recommended to managers, makers of regional policy and other researchers?

Questions 1, 2, 3 and 5 will be answered principally in chapters 2, 3 4 and 7 respectively. Question 4 will be dealt with in chapters 5 and 6.

"I saw one once," said Piglet. "At least, I think I did," he said.
"Only perhaps it wasn't."
"So did I," said Pooh, wondering what a Heffalump was like.
(Winnie-the-Pooh)

CHAPTER 2   SIX LOCALIZATION PROCESSES

Six case studies of location decision processes, based on informal
interviews, are described in detail.

2.1   Introduction to Six Location Decision Processes

The main conclusion so far is that in the light of the present state of
knowledge, it is not very fruitful to direct research toward particular
variables and their partial relationships. What is needed is a "systems
view". In other words we need to find out how the whole system operates and discover its major properties. Since my review of the literature did not result in the discovery of any major properties besides
the conclusions that the location decision is only one of an array of
decisions and the problem is low programmed, ill-structured and difficult to validate, I felt it necessary to interview people directly involved in location processes.

To be more precise, the purposes of this investigation were first to
describe the phenomenon of location planning in great detail and secondly to identify the forces affecting the behaviour of those involved in such
situations. In order to do this, a number of specific case-studies will
be examined.

17

In using the case-study method when constructing theories I am following a number of social scientists, e.g. Glaser & Strauss (1967) and Normann (1973). As Normann puts it, this method "seems better suited than the first" - (i.e. the traditional method used for statistical hypothesis testing) - "for the study of complex social systems and events which are all unique and which - because of their systemic character - have to be considered as wholes" (ibid., p. 50). I might add that in a later chapter in this study, I will also use statistical methods.

During 1971 three Swedish firms, Sandviken, Fagersta and Trelleborg, were studied. At that time Sandviken had just located two branch plants, one to Bollnäs and one to Sveg, while Fagersta had established one branch in Östersund. Trelleborg had far-reaching plans to relocate one of its plants in Östersund, though no formal decision had been made. All the Swedish location decisions studied are thus branch operations. In addition they all came about as a result of labour shortages in the area surrounding the parent company. This field study was documented as an inter-firm comparison in Söderman (1971). During spring 1973 two English establishments were also examined. Oliver Ltd had moved their plant from London to Barnstaple in Devon in order to develop new products in a new industry within a Development Area. During 1975 L'Oreal will move its total production from Leighton-Buzzard in Bedfordshire to Llantrisant in South Wales, a move prompted by the difficulty of obtaining government approval for expansion in Bedford, which is regarded as an overdeveloped area. A more elaborate version of the L'Oreal case than the one presented below can be found in Söderman (1973).

The identification of the Swedish cases was done on a subjective basis by a director of the Federation of Swedish Industries (Industriförbundet). He also put me in contact with potential respondents in the firms and legitimated the study. A research fellow at the Oxford Centre for Management Studies provided similar help with the British cases.

The regional policies of Sweden and England are quite similar and in all of the six investigated cases the incentive schemes offered by the government were used by the companies.

The research was carried out by studying existing documents and conducting informal interviews. Each interview was recorded except for the final hour of discussion. After switching off the tape-recorder I got the impression that the respondents felt a psychological relief and therefore became more talkative. Every interview lasted between four and eight hours. The average number of respondents per firm was two and in most cases these persons could also be regarded as the key actors in the location planning process.

I used an interview guide consisting of key words and short questions. The guide was based on the fragmentary conceptual framework developed in chapter 1 and in particular the paragraphs covering cases of localization processes. The key words will be found in the subheadings of the cases below.

In order to reveal the real inner driving forces the respondents were very seldom interrupted during the talk. Immediately after the interview the case was written up using both my notes and the recordings. The protocol was then sent back to the respondents for checking and correction (except in the Oliver case). This unstructured method of data collection produced quite dissimilar descriptions of the location planning processes. Very different aspects of the problem were emphasized due to the personal views of each respondent.

The cases described below are fairly long. This is unavoidable if we are to obtain a total view of the system and hence understand the phenomenon of location planning. In addition much of the analysis which follows is based on specific data from these descriptions. The identities of all those mentioned in the cases have been concealed by using fictitious names.

The six cases are presented in five sections, since Sandviken was involved in two location planning processes. The order of presentation is quite random.

2.2   The Case of Oliver

Background

The company is about 90 years old, family owned and employing 150 people. Until 1966 it formed part of the rubber industry. At the time its products were bags and, predominately, rubber gloves. In addition there was a small sewing and plastic department employing about 20 people. The company was situated in East London. Parts of its factory were very old and its 30,000 square feet of manufacturing space was badly utilized.

Awareness of imbalance

In 1966, two people, both with considerable experience from the rubber industry, were employed by the company and given the task of modernizing it. Gillespie had previously worked in manufacturing and Jennings, who came three months later, in sales. They did not know each other and neither of them had experience of relocation. The new executives immediately started to "sort things out". They looked at the workforce, the equipment, the markets, the factory and so on and soon realized that new capital investment was necessary for survival.

The rubber gloves industry was at that time dominated by **three** companies (and today by one company). Since they knew this industry well they decided to find out which part of the company would have a future. They found that, principally due to the competitive position of the company, it was impossible to finance an automated plant. The next decision was to concentrate on sewing, plastic and the welding side. Gillespie and Jennings then produced a plan and recommended that the major shareholders accept it and provide the necessary capital. It was decided to sell the plant and locate the new type of production facility in a Development Area. Not long after the subsequent move the two executives also became shareholders.

The decisions were taken in the following order: First it was decided to leave the rubber industry, then to go into the plastic industry by diverting the small department for sewing of plastic goods and lastly to discontinue production in London.

Adjustment and kind of location

The two executives concluded: "... we could not be competitive at that plant with that product". Having decided that, a desk investigation was started concerning the location of the new productive unit. There were no real attempts to avoid change or make any partial adjustments.

Search process; knowledge about alternative locations; company personnel involved

The decision to move was taken a couple of months after Jennings was employed by the company in London. After this the two executives started the search for the new plant without any consultants. They decided that six months was a reasonable time for the planning and searching. Both travelled to look at potential sites. Gillespie probably looked at more sites than Jennings, who at that time was fairly busy in keeping the old business going and also in finding new business ideas. During this first period of time, monthly budgets and a "keen system of costing" were developed and implemented in the firm.

The critical location factor was the labour situation. The way of conducting the search can be summarized in these words of Jennings: "... we do not have, in this small firm, all the experts who know all the sophisticated techniques and we tend to wear several hats. But we are on the other hand trying to look at things sensitively and therefore we looked at the labour position and at the likely requirements for the coming five years."

Concerning raw material - another location factor - it was calculated that a 20 % larger stock would have to be carried since things cannot be brought as quickly into the Development Areas. This naturally requires both more space and more capital.

The third location factor was Government assistance. To apply for this is a very complicated process. The applicant must provide a great deal of information and submit the books of his company to independent inspection by an accountant. The "case" then goes to the Department of Trade and Industry and is put before a panel. If the panel judges the case suitable for assistance the company can get loans, in addition to grants, from the Government; in certain circumstances these even cover items like working capital. There are also special depreciation schemes under which equipment can be written off much more quickly within the assisted areas than elsewhere. These grants and loans are based on a percentage of the total cost. The percentages vary between buildings and machinery and are frequently revised by the Government. The company has the right to get assistance as soon as it is judged to be "suitable".

Requirements

The basic location factor in this case was the availability of female labour. After that it was considered very important to find a place where there had been sewing industry before. The next consideration was Government assistance. The fourth requirement concerned room for expansion. None of these criteria and constraints were formally written down.

Selection/rejection of alternatives

Jennings and Gillespie visited all Government-assisted regions, at that time about six different areas. They looked in Scotland, in Ireland, in Wales and in a couple of places in the North of England. Then the search was concentrated to Devon and Cornwall.

Altogether 20 - 25 places were visited and rejected, some of which were bare lots and some existing factories. The alternatives were discarded one at a time. Within the category of factories some were built by the Government "on spec". In Scotland they both visited six places. They went as far north as Inverness. They were offered a factory in Aberdeen that they turned down since the female labour in the area was principally employed in gutting fish. "We did not think that a woman used to gutting fish was very likely to become a good machinist", Gillespie explains.

They did not want to train too much new labour in the beginning. Other arguments for rejecting locations were: some factories were too large, one or two were too old, some were too far from town. In each case there were specific reasons for rejection. During these travels, the difficulties with being in Scotland in comparison with the South or the Southwest were realised.

At the beginning of their search they went to the Government department and were provided with plenty of literature on possibilities in each area. They were then put in contact with an official in the respective area. After specifying their requirements, a tour of the available factories and sites was arranged. "So in fact you use Government assistance which is not just money. They have a fair knowledge of what is going on." In addition they consulted their own trade association.

Two or three possibilities in the West Country were examined. Barnstaple, the last alternative investigated, was the location finally selected. Glove making has been a traditional industry in Barnstaple for a hundred years. In addition Jennings knew something about this part of the country since he had been at school in the area during the war. He said about the inhabitants: "They are basically hardworking people, pretty honest, and more reliable than Londoners."

Jennings and Gillespie examined the population distribution by age and sex for the area. The competition for labour was fairly light at this time and Oliver was one of the first ten companies to locate in Barnstaple.

The move

A meeting of the employees of the London factory was called and the decision to move was announced. They were all opposed to the closing down of the business. Although jobs were offered in the new plant in Devon, no member of the workforce accepted this offer.

The law provides workers with a redundancy payment based on length of service. A portion of this is paid by the company and the balance by the Government. Jennings was not worried about the workforce: "We paid whatever redundancy was necessary and they all got three job offers for the next day."

The two executives then went to the local office of the Ministry of Labour in Barnstaple and advertized for labour. 50 people turned up for the original jobs and 12 were picked out for training. The old fire station of the town became the training centre. These trainees were later made the nucleus of the labour force. Throughout this period the diverted sewing department in the London factory was kept in operation.

During the next four or five months, the factory was built on the new site that had been bought earlier. When the factory was ready, four key workers (cutters and art mechanics) moved down from London. One came from the old factory and the other three were newly recruited. The London plant was then closed. There were about 20 employees when production started in the new factory. The Government paid 80 % of the costs for the move.

Performance

Having changed from one industry to another Jennings had to do all the marketing himself. At first it was very hard; mainly due to the attitude of the larger customers. They seemed to be more impressed by titles and reputation. "But now we have a good reputation and we sell out six months ahead".

Soon after the move the two executives became directors and could formulate the policy of the company. The board today consists of Jennings, Gillespie and two others "not generally in the business". A company secretary, a former accountant, was also employed. Gillespie thus looked after the production and general affairs, Jennings looked after marketing and sales promotion, while the secretary was responsible for finance.

The predicted problems with the raw material supply gradually decreased. "You tend to cope with such problems" as Jennings put it "... they seem rather difficult at first but you gradually get to find ways and means to handle them."

Originally female labour was fairly easy to get but after a time the supply became much more limited. At the time of the interview (1973) Oliver were preparing to tackle this problem by employing women on a part-time basis and opening a nursery for their workers' children. It is important, Jennings said, to have the reputation of being a reasonable employer. "As soon as rumours get around in the town that they don't like the firm, you can't get the people." After the site was selected it was discovered that most female labour lived on the same side of the river as the new plant, which subsequently proved to be important.

In 1971 the demand exceeded the production capacity and an expansion was planned. However, a nation-wide recession during the winter of 1972 caused the plans to be postponed for about seven months.

The turnover approaches £ 400,000 per year with about 100 employees. The management of Oliver is satisfied with a production figure of £ 4,000 per employee and says" ... not bad in this labour intensive industry".

23

The product range has expanded and the products are now concentrated towards semi-plastic goods: baby pants, garments for medical use etc. Concerning the customer Jennings said: "We work for a lot of famous names and sell them under our own."

"Environmentally this is better than most of the Development Areas, although it has become more fashionable since we came here", Jennings and Gillespie said. Jennings very strongly stresses the problem of assimilation by the environment and the importance to establish links and relations with the local people. Gillespie and Jennings thus made a point of getting involved in local affairs. They formed the North Devon Manufacturers Association of which Gillespie became the first chairman. Jennings became involved in the Chamber of Commerce and was elected its president in 1968. Gillespie also belongs to the Town Council and the South West Economic Planning Council in Bristol representing small businesses. Through these activities both have got to know a lot of people in North Devon. As Jennings says: "We are trying to give something back to the area as well as taking something out."

The turnover has been multiplied by four since production started in 1966. There is capacity to increase the turnover to £ 600,000 and there is room to expand. But money and people are required for such an expansion.

In retrospect it is always easy to say it was a correct location decision. But Jennings and Gillespie seem very pleased and are not willing to go back to London. With some minor exceptions all the targets formulated before the move, including plans and budgets, have been achieved.

2.3   The Case of Fagersta

Background

The company of Fagersta AB evolved from the merger between about five ironworks at "Bergslagen" during the late 1920´s. Fagersta has since then grown to one of the largest steelworks in the country with more than 6,000 employees (1970) in Sweden. The head-quarters are in the municipality of Fagersta in Västmanland county and the production units are situated around the original ironworks.

Awareness of imbalance

In 1966 Fagersta´s management decided to make a major effort to expand a particular product range and a strategic plan to carry out this decision was drawn up. Products within this range were at that time manufactured in the main plant in Fagersta as well as in a wholly-owned branch in Sweden. In accordance with the new plan parts of two competing firms involved in the same field were taken over and successively transferred to Fagersta. By 1969 they were fully incorporated. Until 1970 the aim was to keep all production within this special field concentrated in these two places, since it was calculated that labour supply could be expanded at the same rate as the growth in product demand.

However, in 1970 a new long-range plan, covering the six years up to 1976, showed that neither Fagersta nor the branch would be able to recruit enough labour to permit the planned expansion to take place. The plan estimated that 500 - 600 new employees would be required over a five year period, whereas the official regional plans predicted that only 300 - 400 people within the area would seek employment during this period of time. Furthermore, half of these traditionally sought employment in the service sector and local industry would thus have to compete for the remaining 150 - 200. The branch factory also needed a considerable amount of labour: 300 people within three years.

These needs would be impossible to satisfy and the planned expansion could not take place, even though Fagersta had procured well-sized plots in both sites. The 1970 long-range plan was mainly based on two facts. First, the exceptional demand for the products in question during 1970, especially during the summer, and secondly, the fact that in the spring of 1969 Fagersta had signed an agreement to collaborate with a leading American firm. This resulted in increased demand.

Attempts to adjust and kind of location

Since 1920 Fagersta had pursued an explicit policy of sticking to the places where it was already established. In order to increase its capacity it had to abandon this policy. Fagersta also owns some ten factories outside Sweden, but did not consider location abroad as an alternative in this case.

Setting up the organization

Fagersta did not have a permanent department for location planning. The possibility of building a new plant was discussed by management, who also tried to find out which executives had contacts that could be useful. One of Fagersta´s ten executives, Mr Hagen, a graduate engineer and the representative to whom I talked, assumed the responsibility. A small committee was appointed to examine the problems more thoroughly than would have been possible if the whole of management had been involved. The committee consisted of Hagen who is the head of the expanding department, the administrative director who is also head of personnel, and the director of investments.

Location requirements and objectives

Fagersta did not formulate any restriction on the location of the site before the search began. The spokesman for Fagersta claimed that the goals of the company were embodied in its long-range plan which had been accepted by the board. These goals were expressed in terms of turnover, result, and range of products.

Management, according to Hagen, made statements like "we want a good environment for the workers". No goals were formulated in writing, however, and he did not take such statements too seriously.

Labour

The greatest importance was attached to what would happen in five years, when Fagersta might need 300 workers. If this were then impossible the situation would be more severe than before the location decision was taken. Regional disequilibria in supply and demand of labour are smoothed out because "the world is shrinking" and people are increasingly mobile. Hagen holds this to be especially true for Mälardalen and the southern parts of Sweden. All of Mälardalen will have scarce labour during the seventies, resulting in high wage levels. Hagen thinks labour will be available only during times of economic recession. Discussions within the management of Fagersta led to the conclusion that it would not be wise to locate in a small place in Småland, where 100 workers plus a factory building were available. In northern Sweden the mobility is considerably lower and Fagersta's representative further believes that the local people have a strong desire to remain in these parts, or to return as soon as possible if they are forced to leave.

As a result of these discussions, management agreed to look for alternative locations in the north. At this point no attempts had been made to estimate the cost of production start-up.

Cost of transport and time

Hagen states that transport costs mean very little for the manufactured goods in question - only a few öre per unit. Practically everything is transported by road nowadays. The branches receive their raw material from other branches of the company.

Finance

Fagersta's experience highlighted the fact that larger companies enjoy a comparative advantage is their dealings with the Government. Society - in the form of the authorities - treats the smaller companies differently; their applications are handled much more slowly and so on. "When locating this branch we found that Östersund and Kiruna were the only cities attractive to us within the inner Development Area where maximum grants were given. There was a small economic factor in favour of these two places."

Search process

Hagen studied the file of documentation published jointly by the Federation of Swedish Industries and the Ministry of Labour and Housing (Industriförbundets och Inrikesdepartementets pärm). According to Hagen, these contained enough valid data to answer their questions without their having to visit the areas.

Despite this, however, a number of places in Jämtland were visited during the summer of 1970. Personal contacts with the local authorities played an important part. Fagersta studied other companies which had located in the place that was later selected, and the time it had taken for these companies to recruit labour. The companies were not questioned directly. Hagen made a second trip accompanied by the managing director who accepted the site suggested.

As to the existence of a "data bank", Hagen said that the investment department collect certain information but not specifically regarding location. Technical data on production are well documented.

Selection/rejection of alternatives

"Lokaliseringsbyrån" continually published reports, one of which was noticed by the management in Fagersta at the time of the initial discussions about a new location. It was decided to contact Lokaliseringsbyrån, which presented a list of companies being closed down, empty plants, and companies which were looking for a new owner and could be restructured. In collaboration with this organization, Fagersta investigated some alternatives in Jämtland. The firms listed were also located in Småland, Västergötland, and Dalsland. No further alternatives were investigated. As previously explained alternatives outside the north were eliminated because of the labour supply situation. Discussions led to agreement on the advantages of the site at Östersund and this was selected. This agreement was almost entirely based on the supply of labour. One further comparison was made between the selected site and some larger towns along the coast of Västerbotten and Norrbotten, but these alternatives were eliminated on the grounds that enough industry was already located in them. Hagen also said that the municipality officials were active and helpful in presenting plans, designs and maps. The different factors involved in the locations were not quantified since "the differences between the alternatives were so evident that this was not necessary". However what Hagen calls a "standard calculation" was made. "This was possible because one knows by experience how much things cost and what the results will be. This calculation showed that the project would be profitable wherever located."

The final choice and the future plan

The board of directors of Fagersta accepted the Östersund site on condition that the Government would grant a location subsidy. In November 1970 this request was granted. The cost of the plant was estimated at 12 million Skr, 67 % of which was met by Government subsidies i.e. a combination of location grant and loan.

It was planned to carry out the erection of the new plant in Östersund in a number of phases. The first phase would provide the experience and form the nucleus for the rest of the construction. People from all over the country applied for the top posts. Half of the applicants were from the northern parts of Sweden. The wage-earners were recruited locally as usual. Production was due to start in March 1971 (the interview was held in January 1971) with 15 workers, a couple of foremen and an engineer. Another 15 employees were being trained. It was planned that, two years after start-up, the plant would employ 100 - 110 people, including a staff of 20.

2.4 The Case of L'Oreal

Background

Production started in the mid 1940's on a very small scale in Leighton-Buzzard, in Bedfordshire. The firm, Golden Ltd grew very fast, and a new plant was required and built. Production on this new site, within walking distance of the old one, started in 1964.

Golden Ltd are now manufacturers and distributors of the products of L'Oreal, a worldwide company. L'Oreal has factories in many European countries, e.g. in Belgium, Holland, Denmark, Finland and 10 - 20 plants in France. Golden Ltd is controlled financially from the head office in Paris, but in practice operates very autonomously, since the production is market oriented and therefore many decisions must be taken in response to local market conditions. The policy has thus been to put the factory in the middle of the market, i.e. roughly one factory per country (except for France). But the basic products are the same throughout the whole of Western Europe. The R & D facilities are now in the Paris area, with no R & D in England.

Golden Ltd is a public company and the stock is almost totally French-owned (99.9 %). (This is the reason for calling the case L'Oreal rather than Golden Ltd.) The majority of the stock is probably owned by one family.

At the time of the interview sales were growing at around 15 % p.a., and the turnover was between £ 8 and £ 10 million. Profits were also increasing, but obviously fluctuating from year to year. There were 450 employees in Leighton-Buzzard. The company produced 700 different products all of which were classified as either cosmetics or toiletries. Every year 10 - 20 new products were introduced. Golden Ltd said of their products: "They lie in the high quality end of the market - and are very expensive." "We are in the luxury market to a certain extent. The top of the expensive section of the mass market."

The number of competitors differed between product lines. In hair dyes, there was one large competitor in each of Germany and England. In hairsprays, Golden Ltd was small and the main companies were probably Unilever and Beecham plus Colgate (these firms all have factories in England). In shampoos, Golden Ltd was very small and the big competitors again Unilever and Beecham.

Awareness of imbalance

The company has rolling five-year plans that are renewed each year. These start with sales forecasts or an evaluation of what "market requirements are likely to be". Demand for each of the products is thus forecast. Investment decisions concerning machinery are made two years in advance. Every year new machines are bought for different products, including new products, e.g. in changing over from metal tubes to plastic tubes, new machinery has to be bought. These plans showed that within a few years Leighton-Buzzard's total capacity would not be sufficient to meet the requirements.

In 1969 the head of the Golden Ltd plant in Leighton-Buzzard, the general works manager Mr Peters, realized that within three or four years the plant was likely to reach the saturation point. (This view was confirmed by the passage of time. By May 1973 the plant was overloaded.) He also realized that the plant was situated in an area where it was difficult to get the right sort of labour at the right price. Peters was the first to become aware of the problem and he was the key man in pushing it in the early stages. However, though he came to work on it at a later date, as soon as it was seen as a company problem, it was handled by company representatives from Golden Ltd's head office in London.

Search process and people in company involved

No explicit procedure was formulated for carrying out the search. No budget was established nor was any time limit fixed beyond the rather vague requirement that: "something has to happen before 1974".

Peters, who was educated as an accountant, the managing director, Vidal, and his assistant from London worked on the relocation problem. Staff from both places also assisted in the search procedure, but no formal group was given the task of solving the problem.

Attempts to adjust and kind of location

Golden Ltd owns a lot of land at the back of the existing factory. When the plant was completed in 1964 it was thought that it would be able to expand. Subsequently Government regional policy was altered and Golden Ltd was not allowed to use this land for expansion. Government approval in the form of an Industrial Development Certificate, is required for the building of new facilities. (This is similar to the system proposed in SOU 1974:82 and the newly suggested Swedish government authority "Statens lokaliseringsdelegation".) "Either approval was refused or we were told that it would be refused if we asked." The Department of Trade and Industry issues permission to erect a new building providing its purpose meets with their approval. New warehouses are sometimes allowed in Bedford, although it is regarded as an overemployed area.

Peters made his own investigation with the idea of changing production schedules in the existing plant to avoid a complete removal. It was, however, difficult to increase output by making new capital investments, because of the great number and very wide range of products. The machines were operated over a wide range of tasks. Some of the machines were used on the line for only an hour or even half an hour, after which they had to be cleaned (an operation that could take up to two hours). Thus it did not make a significant difference if a few minutes were saved by using machinery with a somewhat higher capacity. There were, however, some lines where capacity could be increased by using new machines - where the lines ran more continuously. The problems of inventory control could have been solved separately by hiring a warehouse. Hypothetically "we could produce fewer of the small items". Instead of producing 700 items, 100 high-volumed items could be produced. This would allow the company to install much more powerful machines. Profit might be increased if fewer of certain items and more of others are produced. However, this is not Peters´ problem. He is simply told what he must produce.

Despite these considerations it was decided that the best solution would be to build a new factory. The principal advantages of this would be:

a) Production would not be disrupted in Leighton-Buzzard

b) The potential risk of labour problems should not be as great for complete relocation.

The main disadvantage with a new factory is the need for duplication of management. Against a complete transfer is the redundancy compensation which will cost the company a lot, but which seems to be the accepted practice in similar cases in England.

The alternatives were:

1. To close the plant in Leighton- Buzzard and build a much bigger one elsewhere, or

2. Build a smaller one elsewhere and keep Leighton-Buzzard.

The first alternative was selected, but very late, and after the search for sites was finished. The decision meant that all machinery from Leighton-Buzzard plus part of the head office from London had to be moved to the new plant.

Location requirements

Golden Ltd´s main objective in its early years, had been to maximize growth in sales, though profit maximization is probably the present objective. However no formal statements about goals exist. The objective of the relocation is apparently to minimize disturbances for the company or minimize costs, but nothing is explicitly formulated. A number of requirements, however, were drawn up:

a) The site should be in a Development Area since cash support from the Government would defray part of the relocation costs.

b) The area should contain some reserves of labour, primarily unskilled.

c) Good communications with the South East - the major market.

d) Good communications - in terms of distance and travelling time- with the Channel Coast. A major portion of the company´s raw materials, packaging components etc., comes from France.

e) Good communications with London - the head office.

f) Good housing, schools, hospitals and other amenities.

g) The site itself had to be flat and easy to build on.

h) Since there is an image of beauty involved with a cosmetic factory, the site had to be attractive.

From Altham to Llantrisant

The Department of Trade and Industry organizes visits to Development Areas. City corporations also contacted Golden Ltd and suggested available sites. The company looked at "all they could look at". Besides the North of England, other areas, primarily Cornwall and South Wales, were considered. In 1970 the company took an option to purchase a plot of land at Altham, North Lancs, with the purpose of building a second factory. Plans and designs for this factory were produced and the contractors appointed.

However, the Government changed the size of cash grants for Development Areas. South Wales then became more suitable than Lancashire. Changes in the transport system also created incentives for a new search. "The rail communication to London was not very good three or four years ago, but has since improved, and there is now a motorway link to South Wales."

Peters and Vidal, the managing director, went off to look at South Wales more intensively without committing themselves to Lancashire. The representatives at Golden Ltd decided that the northern area in South Wales was not suitable for industrial development. Though the closure of many of the coal mines and old fashioned steel mills has resulted in high unemployment in this area, it consists principally of long, narrow valleys which result in bad communications. For this reason it was decided to look in the more pleasant Glamorgan area, i. e. south of the coalfields. New industries are growing in these flat areas.

There was, however, a very limited choice and enormous difficulties in finding "good" industrial sites. Half a dozen sites were considered superfically and all these were more or less consciously compared with the Altham site. They were all rejected. However, one further site was considered in great detail and was finally selected.

Peters and Vidal went around in a car searching for sites and passed a field with nice surroundings in Llantrisant. They asked the farmer if he was prepared to sell it, and started to negotiate with him. Golden Ltd bought the field in 1971.

Labour

Although the valley area is generally not suitable for industry an attempt is now being made to locate new light industries in the area to the immediate south of the valleys, and to encourage the unemployed in these valleys to move out. The whole area has roughly

1 million inhabitants of whom 7 - 8 % are without jobs. These former coal miners and steel workers live in an industrial area where the industrial revolution began. Younger people are moving south while the older workers tend to commute since they cannot afford to move. Golden Ltd plans to employ 400 people to start with, of whom a large proportion will be commuters and will spend two hours a day in their cars. The company thinks there is a sufficient pool of labour in the area of the kind which is required. On top of this, the industries in South Wales predominantly employ men and half of Golden Ltd's labour force is female. It is not intended to employ part-time workers.

Golden Ltd receives training grants, but the amount is secret since the company has to negotiate with the Department of Trade and Industry. If a person is brought down from Leighton-Buzzard to Llantrisant to set up the factory, the company gets a grant. Golden Ltd thus gets money for the "nucleus labour force" or "key workers" - without whom the factory could not run.

There is also another kind of training grant. If Golden Ltd brings a person up from South Wales to Leighton-Buzzard, the company can make a request to the Department of Employment and Productivity for part of the costs incurred in bringing him (or her) to Leighton-Buzzard, and then some money can be drawn from the Government. The employees do not get any money direct from the Government themselves. A key worker can also get a council house. If he is not a key worker, he has to go on a waiting list; that is the general case with management people. However, Llantrisant has good physical amenities. "To get management to move, one has to offer them something good."

Finance

Golden Ltd also gets "building grants" of 45 % as well as "plant and machinery grants" öf 22 %, which are paid in cash. The company can, if it so desires, depreciate the plant and machinery 100 % in the first year. No loans have been taken from the Government as far as was known.

Transport

The authorities plan to build a motorway in the flat area near Glamorgan. North of this area communications are bad, and will continue to be bad in the foreseeable future. Golden Ltd use contractors to transport raw materials and finished products in the same manner as they now do in Leighton-Buzzard, since this system is found to be the most economic. The

finished products are distributed to the clients through a number of
warehouses and depots scattered around the country.

Sources and consultants

When a large employer - at full capacity Golden Ltd has 1,000
employees in Llantrisant - has relocation problems, it gets a "tre-
mendous amount of help" from the Government and, in this case, from
the Welsh office. During the process Golden Ltd has obviously had
contacts right up to the top of the Department of Trade and Industry.
In Golden Ltd the contact men were Vidal and Peters (and eventually
their staff as well).

The company has also bought services from a small firm who helped
the company to make contact and deal with various Government bodies.
Golden Ltd was thus always introduced by this firm, which probably
did not have anything to do with selecting sites.

Concluding remarks and the final decision

"Line people" seem to have done the main planning in this relocation.
The costs for visits were apparently small. No similar relocation
had been conducted in England before, and there is no experience of
such problems. The Group in Paris has, however, located many
factories and certainly gave Golden Ltd a lot of help during the planning process.

The final decision was taken in the head office in Paris during 1971.
London actually presented two alternatives - Altham and Llantrisant
- with a strong recommendation for the latter. L'Oreal Group selected
Llantrisant but also decided to concentrate all production facilities in
South Wales together with certain of the administrative departments
from London, instead of the earlier proposal to build a smaller additional unit and keep the Leighton-Buzzard factory.

The problem was discovered	in 1969
The plot of land in Altham was bought	in 1970
The plot of land in Llantrisant was bought	in 1971
The final decision was made	in 1971
The employees in Leighton-Buzzard were offered redundancy and compensation if they followed the company	in 1973

Planning after the final decision but before the move

Taylor was appointed the internal coordinator within the Leighton-Buzzard factory in September 1972 and retained this position until June 1974. Taylor was the company representative to whom I talked. As an assistant to Peters, he was responsible for planning and carrying out the move. He thus controlled the different managers in getting the "right information" and saw to it that the detailed planning work was done. There was also a man with a similar function in London who worked on these tasks full-time.

It is not feasible in this industry to change techniques just because of a relocation. Hence the move does not affect the product lines at all. Existing machinery is simply taken to pieces and transported to Llantrisant.

The move is phased in thirds, and the company loses a third of its production capacity during the time the machines are out of action. One third of the productive output is lost in each of three six-week periods. These occurred roughly in July 1973, October 1973 and in June 1974.

In February 1973 the employees were offered redundancy schemes. Everybody who wants to go to Llantrisant would get a job there. Golden Ltd gives everybody £ 400 tax free to cover refurnishing, carpets etc. Everyone is also offered a six months salary bonus - tax free - as a further incentive. Of the 450 people in Leighton-Buzzard, 90 said they were interested in moving. Some of them have since changed their minds. Taylor thinks 45 will eventually make the move, most of whom will be staff.

2.5 The Sandviken Cases

Background

The company was established during the 1860´s and, like Fagersta, manufactures steel. The production units are concentrated in the town of Sandviken in Gävleborg county. Sandvik-Koncernen, which is currently the company´s correct name, had about 10,500 employees in Sweden in 1970. The company has built one branch in Bollnäs, where production started in 1968 and another branch in Sveg, where production started in September 1970. These cases will be described.

Awareness of imbalance

Sandviken used to work with continual five-year plans but has now changed to four-year plans + eight-year outlines. The four-year plan is based on a forecast of demand by all sales units (Sandviken has daughter companies in Sweden and abroad). The capital needed to provide the capacity to meet this demand is then calculated. During the last few years only plans for expansion have been made. The plan also comprises a budget and short surveys on the supply of other resources such as labour. It emphasizes the importance of investments for rationalization to increase productivity and reduce the dependence of labour. The need for expansion is explicitly stated but without details as to how, when and where. The four-year plan current at the time the interviews for this study were made (January, 1971), stated that the number of employees at Sandviken had to be increased by 1,000 by 1974. During the preceding four-year period intense recruitment efforts only resulted in 400 new employees, all of them women. In spite of efforts to attract workers, and in particular female workers, through such alternative employment schemes as part-time work, the planning of a new branch was considered necessary.

Attempts to adjust and kind of location

When faced with a problem of growth, it is Sandviken's policy to ask the question: shall the main plant be expanded or part of it transferred, i.e. a division or a product split off from the main plant? It is then decided whether the new plant should be erected in Sweden or abroad. The aim is to take one kind of production from the main plant at Sandviken and locate it where expansion is unrestricted. This kind of location approach is accompanied by rationalizations, such as the purchase of new machinery and the adoption of new production methods. The representative from Sandviken emphasized the difficulty of predicting the trends of demand and thus the necessary adjustments in capacity.

Setting up the organization

A supervisor, Dalberg, is responsible for all questions of relocation. He is assisted by Larson, who in turn is in charge of three people who work full-time, two dealing with establishments abroad, and the third, Frid, with locations in Sweden (see figure below).

The supervisor exercises direct control over:

1. negotiations with the Government
2. purchase of land
3. construction of buildings

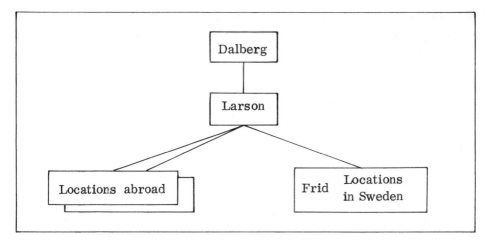

Larson only participates in meetings at which he gives his views; he does not consider himself directly involved in the relocation decisions. But when the site and the starting time for the new unit is fixed, Larson is responsible for the recruitment of personnel and the starting up of production. Dalberg was responsible for most of the location planning for the Bollnäs branch, Larson and Frid had little or nothing to do with this project. Larson and Frid were the people interviewed. Larson is a graduate engineer. Frid, who is older than Larson, is called project leader and has been working full-time with locational questions for about one year.

Location requirements and objectives

No restrictions were formulated before looking for alternatives. Of course, as Larson pointed out, the project was conducted in the light of the company's overall goals which are to maximize profit in the long run and to survive. Management had expressed these goals in writing. The objective of a relocation is to increase production at the rate of demand and to maintain or preferably increase the profitability of the products that have been moved through a process of rationalization. Larson and Frid further recall that the managing director had declared on several occasions that one of the objectives of Sandviken is to guarantee full employment in the places where the company has production units.

Larson considers that, after labour supply and the factors, such as housing, services and schools which affect it, the next most important consideration is transportation. But it is nothing like as important as labour supply. Manufactured products are transported by lorry and the location of the factory is not a problem. But the respondents did stress the importance of being near Sandviken for administrative reasons. "It is expensive for the administration to visit the different places, and it takes a lot of time."

From now on the two case descriptions will be separated. The Bollnäs case is described in the column to the left while the Sveg case is in the right-hand column.

Search process

Before deciding to locate the branch at Bollnäs, Sandviken looked for a place as close to the parent company as possible but with sufficient labour, service facilities, and housing. The extension of the Development Area also played an important role.

This location project was – as has already been mentioned – handled by Dalberg, who used the information contained in an investigation carried by the Governor (landshövding) of the county (Gävleborg) in which Bollnäs is situated.

This official played an important role in the location of the plant. He investigated the supply of labour and the number of job opportunities in the county and contacted Sandviken with a view to procuring subcontracts for the region where the plant was later to be located. Dalberg visited some of the places suggested though no component-manufacturing subcontracts were placed as a result of these visits. However, the Governor and the local authorities of Bollnäs then approached the company again in an attempt to attract employment opportunities. From the investigation that had already been made the company knew that there were sufficient people in the town, which was surrounded by a vast rural area, and that a state-owned engineering workshop located there was going to be closed down in the near future.

Selection/rejection of alternatives

Sandviken did have two alternatives to the Bollnäs site - one in Jämtland and the other in Västerbotten. According to Frid, the company was offered cheap land by the local authorities. These two initial alternatives however were eliminated as a result of the calculation of transport costs. Later Dalberg himself (who was not interviewed) selected the alternative which was chosen (Bollnäs).

Larson recalled that "there was no planning or discussion of the Sveg location, and for a very good reason". Originally it was Sandviken's intention to increase capacity at Bollnäs and thus no other branch was planned. But before he would advance the necessary capital from the investment fund. the Minister of Finance demanded that another branch should be established in a site selected by him and that a specified number of people should be employed at this new plant. Sandviken accepted this condition since it involved a cost representing only a minor part of the amount applied for from the fund.

Finance and the final choice

For the establishment of the Bollnäs factory, and other investments Sandviken was allowed to draw 40 million Skr in 1968. Of this 11.9 million Skr were intended for Bollnäs. Out of the 40 million in the investment fund, 75 % could be used, i.e. 30 million could be drawn from the Riksbank.

In June 1970 Sandviken applied for a further release of investment funds, including the amount needed for Sveg. and got permission from the Minister of Finance three days later. They were allowed to draw 125 million Skr, which covered several projects and investments for the period 1970 - 1973. Only 2 million Skr were intended for Sveg

For new establishments fairly detailed plans are normally drawn up. The move to Bollnäs did not conform with the plan; the transfer of production was delayed because of an economic recession at the time of production start-up. When times got better, production was moved out quicker than planned which resulted in machinery as well as personnel problems. There was no time to work out new contracts for all the workers, which led to insufficient earnings and a large number of resignations. Manufacturing errors proved greater than anticipated, due to the high proportion of inexperienced personnel. In January 1971 there were 130 workers and 15 staff at Bollnäs.

At Sveg the total number of employees was 12. No performance was reported since production had started on a very small scale only a couple of months before the interview.

2.6   The Case of Trelleborg

Background

The final case is based on Trelleborgs Gummifabrik AB. a company in the rubber industry. By the beginning of this century Trelleborg was already one of the largest producers of technical rubber goods in Scandinavia, and by the 1950´s it had become Scandinavia´s largest rubber company. In 1971 the company employed nearly 6,500 people. The headquarters and a large part of the production is concentrated in the municipality of Trelleborg in the county of Malmöhus.

Awareness of imbalance

As already mentioned, Trelleborg had not made a branch location before 1971 (the time of the interview), but in spite of this seemed to have devoted a lot of resources in terms of personnel and time to location planning. It seemed that there were several reasons for

Trelleborg´s desire to establish a new plant in a different area. It was not only the labour situation. This project was included in the five-year plan, in the yearly budget and in the two-year shadow budget.

Attempts to adjust and kind of location

Trelleborg´s basic aim is to remain a Swedish company, although expansion investments are made abroad as well as in Sweden. The respondents did not mention any long-range plan acting as a trigger, but admitted that the situation in the labour market was an important location factor. Trelleborg had expanded over the few years prior to 1971, but capacity had been increased in a specific way. Small firms with liquidity difficulties within a maximum transport distance of two hours had been bought or chosen for collaboration. The idea was to maintain personnel and facilities but to introduce the Trelleborg products and perform the administrative control from the main plant. These small firms were often based on commercially valuable ideas and rational methods. The expansion policy mentioned here is passive and unpredictable since it is based on "suddenly emerging projects". However, it was claimed that the increase in capacity had been based on a systematic search for areas in the region with labour surplus and through investigations of the labour situation.

The company was also open to locations outside Sweden. Branches already existed in Common Market countries and European integration was being watched very closely. The representatives from Trelleborg said that "although it is a Swedish company economic reality might force us to establish abroad". In principle the company considered three location alternatives: (1) branch in Sweden, (2) branch abroad, and (3) acquisition of small firms with liquidity difficulties within the region.

Setting up the organization

During my visit to Trelleborg I talked to Anderberg, who is the head of the department in charge of plants and developments, to Kjellman the project secretary in this department and to Erikson, the director of finance and vice managing director of the company. Anderberg and Kjellman - both graduate engineers - constituted an investigation committee with the task of presenting facts and describing different suitable location alternatives. This information was handed over to the board who made the decision. Kjellman was at that time working on 8 - 10 projects of different size and had been employed at Trelleborg for a couple of months. This project was said to be taking shape; calculations were being made. It was Anderberg who gave the overall presentation of the company's working methods and attitude to this question but Erikson was also very well informed.

Location requirements and objectives

Trelleborg had decided at an early stage that a possible site must have a local labour market of at least 30,000 people. 30,000 was considered big enough for people to remain in the area and to allow for new inhabitants in the near future. A region of greater population was no restriction, but if the region was too heavily populated competition for labour was likely to be too great. The region comprises people living within commuting distance of the site. The size of this area thus depends on population density as well as the quality and quantity of roads and transport facilities. Anderberg emphasized that the location site must be convenient to schools, hospitals, and other social services.

At the time of the interview Trelleborg had not made the final decision on the site. However, they had formulated three alternative goals for a relocation, each of which is expressed through quantified factors related to production. Some of these are:

	Objective 1	Objective 2	Objective 3
Turnover	3.0-3.7 mkr	8 mkr	9.5 mkr
Number of employees	57	114	130
workers, male	30	50	65
workers, female	20	50	50
staff	7	14	15

After start-up the initial intention was to concentrate on labour intensive production. In the longer run the administrative unit would also be transferred, thus making the branch more independent.

Labour

The first assumption Anderberg made was that the further north one moves in Sweden, the more stable the future supply of labour. In the very north it is exceptionally stable since workers are released by the continued rationalization of forestry and agriculture. At that time Nordkalotten - which can be regarded as one labour market - had 1.6 million inhabitants. It was further assumed that Swedish labour would be replaced at an increasing rate by people from Finnish Lapland crossing the border and settling down in northern Sweden. The supply of labour measured in terms of its stability or turnover could be considered as linear and decreasing towards the north. This is shown graphically in the next section on transport cost. Anderberg and Kjellman were aware of the simplifications underlying this assumption since it does not deal with bigger cities where, normally, there is no lack of labour but where, at the same time, mobility and turn-over are often very high. It would also be possible, Anderberg thought, to find a location alternative further south more or less by chance. This would have to be in a place with a stable local labour market and it would pose the problem that many other industries might be attracted to the area. It was further considered that the curves of labour surplus change much more quickly in the southern parts of the country than in the northern. Trelleborg was prepared to locate its plant far up in the north in order to be the sole industry in that place for some time. The reason for this is that the company considered it to be very important that the basic calculations made before the move should be relevant for as long as possible. A misjudgement of the present and future labour situation would cause great trouble since the possibility of moving people to Norrland is considered to be neg-ligible.

The Trelleborg actors also emphasized some important qualitative aspects of the labour supply, such as present and future age range and present employment of men and women in different places. The long-range aspect of the planning and the problems of prediction were stressed on many occasions. "Our recommendations to the board are based on the depreciation of capital over a 15 - 25 year period." It is vital to know the age distribution; a high average age general-ly means lower productivity and may also hamper the provision of service facilities by the local authorities because of the high costs of medical and social care for the old.

A low degree of employment among women is often due to an old-fashioned attitude among the men. This kind of prejudice must be investigated to decide whether it can be changed. This is best done in conjunction with the local authority. Potential female labour can be invited to visit different companies to talk to women who already work and so on.

Trelleborg management stressed the advantage of choosing a site with an industrial tradition, where people are used to fixed hours, shift work, etc. This is a question of attitude and experience, not only with-in the working group but also amongst their families. Getting used to factory work may take a long time; night shift work, for example, changes the routine of the whole family. The school system in Norr-land is good, with a surprisingly large number of secondary and tech-nical schools. Young people emerging from these schools try to get jobs in the big cities since there is usually nothing available in the home region, and the few jobs which do exist are quickly filled by people returning home with practical experience from other parts of the country. This desire of well trained local people to return home was an important factor considered by Trelleborg's management in assessing the possiblity of establishing sophisticated production facilities in Norrland.

Apart from the amount of labour available and the overall industrial experience in the area, the ability of individuals must naturally also be examined. Trelleborg considered two alternative approaches to this problem:

1. To give each employee a training course prior to starting work. This would lead to a faster increase in productivity.

2. To start the employees on production work immediately. The employees must then first of all get used to their industrial surroundings, then train for their jobs and learn to maintain a high level of output. The process would take a long time and those workers who proved unable to adapt would have to be replaced.

Trelleborg made two calculations, one on the basis of untrained labour and the other for retrained labour. Anderberg said that the officials of the National Labour Market Board (Arbetsmarknadsstyrelsen, AMS) appeared to understand the type of training needed, and that the grants were reasonable and attractive. It was thought that the courses would also reveal hidden talents - especially, perhaps, amongst women - who have never had the opportunity of qualified training.

Cost of transport and time

In addition to the "stability of labour", cost of transport and time/ distance were considered most important. The choice of factors was commented on as follows: "We chose some important factors and weighted them. We could just as well have chosen more factors."

The reasons underlying the costs incurred because of the time and distance separating the new plant and the old were explained in the following manner. At that time a semi-manufactured substance was produced at a particular division on equipment which was both expensive and difficult to move. The manufacturing tolerance on this substance was extremely tight, and errors were difficult to detect even in a laboratory. In fact problems only became apparent during the next stage in the manufacturing process, and it was planned to locate this next stage in the new plant. Under these circumstances it is clear

that, in the event of trouble, the total amount of scrap material produced would be directly related to the time which elapsed between the
first faulty batch emerging from the old plant and its introduction into
the next stage of the process at the new plant. In addition the substance
sometimes "ripens" during transit and, again, the total amount of
scrap is a function of the time that elapses between the plants.

There is obviously also a "normal" transport cost related to the distance between the plants. These costs were aggregated and are henceforth referred to as the transport costs. The other cost component,
– stability of labour – is subjectively assessed and expresses the labour
turnover in economic terms. Trelleborg arrived at the model shown
below. The distance from one end of Sweden to the other is measured
along the horizontal axis. The transport costs are assumed to be
zero in Stockholm.

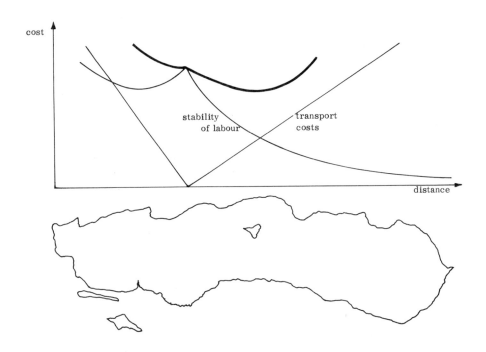

Figure 2:1.   The Trelleborg model illustrates the sum of "transport
                costs" and "stability of labour". The minimum on the
                aggregate curve corresponds to places situated in the
                middle of Sweden.

Finance

The Trelleborg representatives pointed out that in times of restricted credit, financial institutions have only offered investment loans for one part of the country: Norrland. The "entry ticket" for any such discussion appeared to be a site in this part of Sweden. This was considered to be a simplified but realistic picture of the political situation. Anderberg also believed that once a company receives the finance it requires, only a small amount of time is spent in searching for the "best" place for relocation.

Attention was also devoted to the possible duration of the Government subsidies. It was clearly important to work out what would happen if an economic upswing caused the Government to withdraw them. Erikson said that calculations were made on the assumption that the plant would last for 10 years and that the Government subsidies would be withdrawn at an early stage. This led to the elimination of some location alternatives. However, it was generally agreed that subsidies are very attractive and also - in the short run - favourable. Trelleborg therefore made calculations including as well as excluding subsidies.

Search process: New spatial knowledge

The planning undertaken by Trelleborg consisted of two phases, desk research and field research (travels). It was soon realized that no unbiased service for the location of plants was available. The material published jointly by the Federation of Swedish Industries (Industriförbundet) and the Ministry of Labour and Housing (Inrikesdepartementet) as well as the different county plans were acquired and studied. It was felt, however, that these publications did not give appropriate guidance and contained unreliable figures.

The information in the county plans had not been gathered in a systematic way and was badly presented. One of the Trelleborg team said: "The figures are presented with the twofold aim of showing bad results to get money from the Government and good results to attract industries!" Anderberg thought that the information in these plans was "dubious, spoilt and unstructured". Data had been gathered without any scientific methodology. The supply of labour was not described in terms useful to the companies. "The data collectors ought to have tried to imagine what kind of information would be of most use to companies facing a location decision." The information in the plans was not up to date. Firms are continually being closed down and started up and this affects the labour situation. Anderberg solved this problem by studying the basic forecast from 1968 and then interviewing firms and county officials to find out if the surplus of labour had been absorbed or not. The county plans are not comparable. The Ministry of Labour and Housing (Inrikesdepartementet) had failed to coordinate the gathering and presentation of data in different counties.

When the desk research, consisting of the gathering of public information, was finished, Trelleborg representatives travelled around to get some complementary data and to check some facts. Their first trip was planned very thoroughly and the counties to be visited were given notice in advance. The field research consisted of three kinds of contacts:

a) representatives from the County Board
b) local authorities
c) representatives from other companies

The first contact was always the County Board for a presentation of the county. Officials from the Board then accompanied the men from the company when they went to look at the different municipalities. At this point discussions were held with the local authorities, in particular with local authority commissioner (kommunalråd) and deputies of the local building committee (byggnadsnämnd) - but also the director of the housing authority, the local school board, the representatives of the National Labour Market Board (Arbetsmarknadsstyrelsen, AMS), the director of the local employment office and sometimes even the unemployment allowance bureau. The most important discussions concerned population growth. Other subjects covered were water supply, sewage, soil conditions, sites, expansion possibilities and so on. Anderberg asked for site plans, environmental descriptions, the regulations for bomb shelters and also the time necessary for site preparation, the progress of the current city plan and the status of the long-range plans. It often turned out that the local authorities did not know what kind of information a company would require, which meant that it was usually not available and took a long time to produce. Since all companies are bound to ask for the same things, Anderberg came to the conclusion that local authorities should be taught to have this information on hand.

The local authorities were also asked to show the economic calculations for the development and extension of different industrial estates or sites. This is a point on which Anderberg advised caution, since clearly the authorities want to show prospective companies a vast expensive programme and at the same time present a cheap plan to the Board of local authority (kommunstyrelse).

An important experience, which Anderberg mentioned, was that local representatives are very unwilling to admit that recently arrived companies have affected the supply of labour. Furthermore they seem to promise all potential companies the same favours.

It also proved important to find out what the county and the local authorities really thought about industry and to identify the attitudes and the different political stand-points on this issue. Conflicts of interest between county and local authorities can arise as a result of a county's eagerness to attract industry. For example Östersund was at one time quite opposed to industrial expansion although this attitude changed in the mid-1960's.

Finally the Trelleborg team pointed out that they attached great importance to the impression the local representatives made and the manner in which they presented their data.

In each place they visited the Trelleborg representatives tried to find two or three newly arrived firms to learn about their views and experiences. Anderberg asked about their strategy of location, but not one company proved to have systematic experiences. Generally the companies were questioned on how the local authorities kept their promises and what their reaction would be if Trelleborg located in the same area and started competing for labour. The companies interviewed also had advice to give. Thus Trelleborg was discouraged from locating sales departments in Norrland since "the distances are difficult and inconvenient". The location of research and development departments in this region should also be avoided it was said, because of the difficulties in recruiting personnel. The problem which transferred staff have in understanding the mentality of the local workers was pointed out, and Trelleborg was therefore advised to mix their staff so that supervision of the employees would be handled by local staff and technical management by transferred staff. In Anderberg's opinion too few people from the parent plant agree to transfer to the new one. During the initial period the company must of course look after the families of those who have transferred. Anderberg and Kjellman pointed out that these warnings and pieces of advice naturally have a restricted applicability.

The results of the preliminary desk research were confirmed by the field visits. At the time of the interview Anderberg was planning to make a final field trip during which he would evaluate a few more sites in areas he had already investigated.

Selection/rejection of alternatives

Anderberg pointed out that great mistakes might have been made if the basic data had not fitted into the model that was constructed during the desk research phase. Less than 20 sites were selected in this phase. They were then further investigated in the field study. Trelleborg adopted the following procedure: First of all a table was constructed which listed all possible sites in the left-hand column and the follow-ing "control factors" horizontally:

Number of inhabitants 1967
Population growth (%) 1950 - 1967
Number of new housing units 1969 - 1973
Freight transport time from Trelleborg, by rail and by road, in hours
Distance to Trelleborg in kilometres
Passenger transport time from Trelleborg by rail, by car, and by air, in hours
Service facilities - divided into residential, leisure, social, and com-pany - classified either good or poor
Brief descriptions of available education facilities
Structure of industry
Wage level index 1968
Municipality and county tax 1969
Available site in square metres
Larger industries already established
Industries planning to locate

The table was then filled in.

In the next phase some of the control factors were quantified to allow for comparison and evaluation of sites. The methods of quantification, based on a number of different assumptions which appear rather questionable, were highly sophisticated. The factors selected were then weighted and finally added in this scoring model.

The following factors and weights were selected:

Factor	Weight
Supply of labour	10
Construction of housing	2
Freight transport from Trelleborg	4
Passenger transport from Trelleborg	2
Wage level	10
Municipality and county tax	2

This evaluation was followed by a strict investment calculation for a number of alternatives. The zero alternative, i.e. the site where Trelleborg is located at present was compared with all the others.

Erikson stressed the importance of qualifying all the quantitative terms through subjective reasoning since there could be no strictly objective grounds. He further argued that it was necessary to avoid strictly formal analyses in location decisions involving many variables which are difficult to quantify. His experience had taught him that: "mathematical models are much less accurate than common sense. It is essential that one is always fully aware of the assumptions underlying the mathematical calculations. Errors are rapidly magnified through addition and multiplication".

At the time the interviews were made the formal site selection had not been made by the board and accordingly there is no performance to report.

"... It is either Two Woozles and one, as it might be, Wizzle,
or Two, as it might be, Wizzles and one, if so it is, Woozle.
Let us continue to follow them."
(Winnie-the-Pooh)

CHAPTER 3   THE MODELS

In this chapter the research question: "What are the general
variables and factors and how are they related?" will be answered
in three stages. First six variables will be identified, based on
the localization processes of chapter 2. These variables are interrelated and suggest five hypotheses. The variables and the hypotheses constitute the basic model. Secondly the characteristics of
the model are analyzed: the time dimension and the systems level.
Thirdly a second set of forces important when describing the location choice situation are identified. These are referred to as
"factors". 15 factors are identified from the cases in chapter 2
and from the literature. It is argued that these factors affect the
variables through 15 distinct relationships.

3.1   Introduction

When the six localization processes have been described in detail, it is
immediately possible to draw some conclusions concerning certain of
the starting-points from chapter 1.

1.   The decision to adopt a "process approach" rather than a "choice
approach" seems to have been correct. Seldom or never does there

exist only one single choice situation where all the alternatives are identified and the criteria well defined.

2.   The "location factor approach" - that is concentrating on such traditional location factors as the market, transportation and so forth - has also proved to be less useful because of other properties and forces - factors and variables, which have been mentioned as frequently in the cases.

3.   A retrospective analysis was adopted since the study required completed processes (i.e. the final decision must have been made - Trelleborg was an exception). This in turn dictated the use of informal interviews for data collection, a method which theoretically introduces two forms of error - distortion and memory failure. However, I have no reason to suspect any systematic distortion in the six processes and the risk of random distortion was reduced through the procedure of sending back protocols for checking and correction by the respondents. As for memory failure it is probable that some information on unsuccesful steps in the processes went unreported. However it should be noted that the localization processes chosen for study were recent ones and that they were selected because they were interesting to the persons involved; hence, they were fresh in these persons´ minds.

4.   There are in general no distinct steps in the processes of reaching the decision. It is not even possible to determine precise time limits for the activities described under the subheadings in the case.

5.   The conclusions drawn from earlier published case-studies, namely that the location decision is only one of the array of decisions, that it is low programmed, ill-structured and difficult to validate, are to a varying extent confirmed by this study. Although each of the six processes clearly contains unique features there are also some general characteristics which will be described.

Each of the four conclusions above will form the basis for the identification of a set of six variables. These variables express general forces at work in the localization processes described in this study.

6.   Before doing this, however, the terms model, variable and factor need to be further developed and defined (see 8 below).

7.   The use of models for studying problems is common in most sciences. A wide variety of types and classifications of models therefore exists. The model or models to be chosen or constructed in the individual situation depends basically on the role of the model. In certain

contexts the word model is closely associated with activities implying changes of parameter values and the study of subsequent effects. That kind of model presupposes existing sets of variables, and expresses relationships in a mathematical language. In this research, however, two of the main points are, first to identify and describe variables and, secondly, to develop a conceptual scheme. This is necessary before formalized relationships can be developed.

The role of my model is also based on the view expressed by Cyert & March in their well-known behavioral theory published in 1963 (in turn based upon the Marshallian view that (economic) theory is simply a language designed to provide a systematic framework within which to analyze (economic) problems). The words theory and model, when referring to Cyert & March, will be regarded as synonyms. The view is more elaborately expressed in the following quotation by Cyert & March (ibid, p. 114):

> In this view theory performs two major functions. On the one hand, it is an exhaustive set of general concepts. Any variable observed in the system can be assigned to an appropriate niche. The theory is a set of filing cabinets with each drawer bearing the title of an economic concept. Within each file drawer there is a set of folders for each economic variable relevant to the concept. Within each folder there is a further breakdown in terms of the factors affecting the variable. At the same time, the theory is a statement of critical relations among system variables. These relations may be assumptions about interdependence among variables, about the functional form of the interdependences, or about broad structural attributes of the system.

8. Based on this quotation and with regard to the purpose of this study three definitions can now be presented:

1. A model of localization processes is a language designed to provide a systematic framework within which to analyze location problems. The model shall form a basis for the coming field study.

2. A variable constitutes an economic concept in the model.

3. A factor constitutes an economic concept, that affects the variable, in the model.

3.2   Conclusions from the Cases - Identification of Six Variables

I.   It is a conclusion of this study that the rigour with which the lo-
     cation problem is approached is the most important feature of the
     process. It will be referred to as location planning and measured
     by the extent to which knowledge was collected with the explicit
     purpose of selecting a site. The concept of location planning re-
     lates to the conclusion that this kind of problem is ill-structured
     and particularly that the data upon which the selection is based is
     badly defined.

II. In each case there were a number of important decisions made be-
     fore, simultaneous with and/or after the final selection of the site.
     Location choice is only one of the array of decisions although the
     number of other decisions varies. If there are many unmade de-
     cisions before the final choice of site is made, then the situational
     complexity is high, which will reduce the rigour with which the
     site selection is approached.

III. The processes are very much characterized by the individuals in-
     volved and their activities. Earlier it was concluded that these
     processes are low programmed i.e. the actors have generally
     little experience of similar processes, and ill-structured, i.e. the
     criteria on which the choice is based are poorly defined. A large
     number of actors engaged in the location planning will increase the
     rigour with which it is approached.

IV. The distances of the moves vary. To move to a nearby site is one
     way of reducing uncertainty. This conclusion is directly related to
     the one which says that the location problem is low programmed.
     It is also concluded that moves involving large physical distances
     receive more rigourous location planning.

V.   The character of the regional situation including incentives and so
     forth, greatly affects the choice of location. Those company repre-
     sentatives involved with the problem regard the location choice
     situation partly as one of negotiation for subsidies. The negotiation
     contacts with authorities vary. This concept is very closely re-
     lated to the earlier conclusion that the location problem is ill-
     structured including badly defined data. It is concluded that the
     number of negotiation contacts is inversely proportional to the
     rigour of the location planning.

VI. The performance after the move is the sixth and final concept. It
     is concluded in this study that the rigour with which the location
     planning is conducted is related to the performance after the start-

up at the new site. The performance concept is related to the conclusion that the location problem is <u>difficult to validate</u>.

I am fully aware that these six general forces, which from now on will
be referred to as "variables", while they are conceptually related to
conclusions from other case–studies, are based on evidence drawn
from only six localization processes.

Three arguments justify this approach. First, these six concepts are
not new, though they do not seem to have been formally presented in
this manner up till now. Secondly, I do not fully support the view that
a valid hypothesis must produce findings with high probabilities. I
rather take the view which is, perhaps, best formulated by Popper:

> Science does not aim, primarily, at high probabilities. It aims at
> high informative content, well backed by experience. But a hypo-
> thesis may be very probable simply because it tells us nothing, or
> very little.
> (Popper, 1954, p. 146)

Thirdly, I am encouraged in this comparatively minor study by the
knowledge that Cyert & March based their landmark behavioural theory
on just four case–studies.

The six conclusions will now be further substantialized. Within each
case the variables mentioned above will be identified and described.
This will be done in an abbreviated case description. Each variable
is derived mainly from the subheadings in the case descriptions in
chapter 2. The following list shows these derivations:

Variable	Variable number	Mainly derived from the paragraphs headed:
COMPLEXITY	II	The awareness of im-balance
		Attempts to adjust and kind of location
NUMBER OF ACTORS	III	Setting up the organization
NEGOTIATION CONTACTS	IV	Finance
PHYSICAL DISTANCE	V	The final choice
		Location requirements and objectives
LOCATION PLANNING	I	Selection/rejection of alternatives
		Search process: new spatial knowledge
PERFORMANCE	VI	Performance

COMPLEXITY (II): Oliver conducted a systematic decision procedure that led to a final choice of site. First it was decided to leave the rubber industry and go into the plastic industry and then to concentrate on sewing, plastic and welding products. The problems of production technology and kind of location - i.e. here a relocation - were solved by diverting a small department for sewing plastic goods in the London plant. It was then decided to locate the new production facilities in a Development Area. The timing of production start-up was decided at an early stage. Then the two executives started to travel around searching for a suitable site. But the kind of plant (new or old building) was decided later. NUMBER OF ACTORS (III): The two people mentioned conducted all the activities and made all the important decisions preceding the final site selection. NEGOTIATION CONTACTS (IV): The contacts with the authorities were at first indirect and consist-ed of completing application forms. The case was then put before a panel of civil servants and the suitability for assistance was determined. Negotiation contacts were definitively limited. PHYSICAL DISTANCE

(V): The physical distance between London and Barnstaple in Devon is too big to permit one-day visits by car. LOCATION PLANNING (I): The search for sites involved a great deal of travelling. Literature on the possibilities of the different areas was examined and contacts taken with county officers and trade associations. The number of sources consulted seems to have been large. PERFORMANCE (VI): The performance after the move was considered successful. Neither of the two executives wanted to return to London, all the targets (with some minor exceptions) including plans and budgets formulated in advance had been acheived.

COMPLEXITY (II): In Fagersta a lot of decisions seem to have been left unmade during the search for a site. The selection of product, market, capacity, time for production start and kind of location (branch or expansion) seem to have been made simultaneously with the final choice of site. NUMBER OF ACTORS (III): Although a small committee was appointed to examine all the problems of expansion, one person - a top executive - had assumed the overall responsibility of the search for a site. NEGOTIATION CONTACTS (IV): At an early stage the search was directed towards the Development Areas. Location grants and loans were applied for and contacts with the authorities for negotiation purposes can therefore be assumed to be frequent. PHYSICAL DISTANCE (V): The physical distance between Fagersta and Östersund is too great for managers from the mother company to visit the branch by car and return the same day. LOCATION PLANNING(I): Publications from Lokaliseringsbyrån constituted a major source of information together with a "standard calculation" for the investment. Few other people were consulted and the location planning can be judged as limited. PERFORMANCE (VI): At the time of the interview the building on the new site was under construction.

COMPLEXITY (II): In L'Oreal investment decisions are generally made two years in advance since a shortage of capacity can be predicted well in advance. At the time of site selection the product, market, and kind of location have already been decided. NUMBER OF ACTORS (III): People in the company involved in the plant location problem were the general works manager at Leighton-Buzzard, the managing director and his assistant from London as well as staff from both places. NEGOTIATION CONTACTS (IV): Before the final site selection L'Oreal negotiated for training grants with the Department of Trade and Industry and the Department of Employment and Productivity. Besides these negotiations grants for plant and machinery were applied for. Contacts with the authorities thus seem to have been very frequent. PHYSICAL DISTANCE (V): The distance by car between Leighton-Buzzard in Bedfordshire and Llantrisant in South Wales is too great to permit daily visits. LOCATION PLANNING (I): Besides the negotiations with the authorities a number of other sources were consulted during the location planning. Services were bought from a consultant and advice and information from Government and county representatives as well as city trade associations was sought. PERFORMANCE (VI): There is no information on the performance since the move to Llantrisant had not been made at the time of the interview.

COMPLEXITY (II): For <u>Sandviken</u> the choice of markets is made in its long-range plans, but products, capacity, kind of relocation and production technique remain to be determined together with the location site. This general pattern was true for the Bollnäs branch location, but for Sveg several other decisions (capacity, date for production start etc) had already been made when the selected alternative was presented by the Ministry of Finance and immediately afterwards accepted by the company. NUMBER OF ACTORS (III): It seems likely that one person - a supervisor - was responsible for both locations. In the case of Bollnäs however he was influenced by the Governor (landshövdingen) and for the calculations of transport cost he was assisted by some subordinates. NEGOTIATION CONTACTS (IV): In both cases contacts with authorities (on different levels) were frequent and comprehensive and resulted in the release of investment funds. PHYSICAL DISTANCE (V): The physical distance from Sandviken to Bollnäs as well as to Sveg permits managers from the mother company to visit the branch without having to stay overnight. LOCATION PLANNING (I): Unfortunately the main actor for both locations was not interviewed but, according to the representative who was interviewed, the only sources of information that were consulted in the location planning for the Bollnäs case were a report made by the Governor (landshövdingen) and some transport calculations. No other persons seem to have been consulted. For Sveg the amount of location planning was even more limited, since the site was recommended by the Minister of Finance. PERFORMANCE (VI): The move to Bollnäs did not conform with the plan since the transfer of production was delayed and later problems of readjusting the wage system led to insufficient earnings and a large number of resignations. Production at Sveg was about to start at the time of the interview but it was too early to discuss its performance.

COMPLEXITY (II): <u>Trelleborg</u> seems to have decided on product (semi-manufacture), market, production technique, capacity (three objectives), kind of plant and kind of location. The final choice of site however has not yet been made although Östersund seems to be most likely. The time of production start-up also remains to be fixed. NUMBER OF ACTORS (III): At least three people (all interviewed) had been heavily involved in the site selection. NEGOTIATION CONTACTS (IV): Although regional policy had been thoroughly investigated and was emphasized during the interview, no applications for loans or grants had yet been presented. PHYSICAL DISTANCE (V): The physical distance between Trelleborg and Östersund is great. LOCATION PLANNING (I): A large number of sources consulted for the site selection were mentioned, such as county plans and a file of documentation from the Federation of Swedish Industries and the Ministry of Labour and Housing (Industriförbundets och Inrikesdepartementets pärm). Sources of another kind were a transport cost model, a scoring model including a number of weighted factors, and investment calculations. A number of other people were also consulted, especially managers of companies that had located in the areas investigated as well as county and municipality representatives. PERFORMANCE (VI): Since the final choice of the location has not yet been made it is impossible to discuss its performance.

Based on evidence of these six cases the variables can now be defined.

I.   LOCATION PLANNING is defined as the number of sources used – i.e. the number of publications, models and techniques and the people consulted – during the process which ends in a site selection.

II. COMPLEXITY. The decision to select a specific site is a <u>location decision.</u> This decision or choice is preceded by a search process. The location decision, however, is only one of an array of decisions that a company has to make. In the cases above, eight major decisions could be identified, one of which is the location decision. The decisions are as follows:

1. the selection (=decision) of product

2. "   "   "   " market

3. "   "   "   " capacity

4. "   "   "   " production technique

5. "   "   "   " time for production start-up

6. "   "   "   " kind of plant i.e. new/old building

7. "   "   "   " kind of location i.e. new establishment, relocation, branch location

Complexity is defined as the interrelation between the location selection on one hand and the seven other decisions on the other. The degree of complexity is high when none or few of the seven decisions have been taken when the search for a site starts. The complexity is low when a major part of the seven other decisions has been made when the search for a site starts.

III. NUMBER OF ACTORS. The number of people involved in the process preceding the location decision is defined as the number of actors.

IV. NEGOTIATION CONTACTS. In order to acquire financial support from the authorities, the company applies for subsidies. Contacts are made by any of the actors to negotiate grants and loans. The amount of negotiation contacts is defined as the number and duration in hours of contacts with the authorities for negotiation purposes.

V. PHYSICAL DISTANCE is defined as the number of kilometres - by car - between the old and the new site.

VI. PERFORMANCE is defined as the extent to which the success/failure of the location is perceived by the person(s) interviewed.

The variables - as defined above - can now be given values. This is done in all six cases through simple dichotomization and the results are summarized in the table below.

Table of results from the six cases

Name of the case	From	To	COMPLEX-ITY	NUMBER OF ACTORS	NEGOTIATION CONTACTS	PHYSICAL DISTANCE	LOCATION PLANNING	PERFORMANCE
Oliver	London	Barnstaple	low	many (> 1)	few	large	large	success
Fagersta	Fagersta	Östersund	high	few (1)	many	large[1]	small	–
L'Oreal	Leighton-Buzzard	Llantrisant	low	many (> 1)	many[1]	large	large	–
Sandviken	Sandviken	Bollnäs	high	few (1)	many	short	small	failure
Sandviken	Sandviken	Sveg	low[1]	few (1)	many	short	small	–
Trelleborg	Trelleborg	Östersund[2]	low	many (> 1)	few	large	large	–

1/ The result does not support the proposed hypotheses (see section 3.3)

2/ Has not yet been decided, but seems most likely

3.3 The Basic Model

A hypothesis can be based on theories, on empirical evidence (observations) or on a combination of both. In this study the hypotheses originate from empirical evidence based on the six cases already described.

When examining the table of results two kinds of conclusions can be drawn:

1. The variables complexity, number of actors, negotiation contacts and physical distance are related to the location planning;

2. The location planning is related to the performance

These - positive or negative - relations are included in the five hypotheses presented below. They form five general conclusions from this first empirical study.

H 1 (hypothesis 1): The degree of "complexity" is negatively related to the amount of "location planning".

H 2: The "number of actors" is positively related to the amount of "location planning".

H 3: The number of hours for "negotiation contacts" is negatively related to the amount of "location planning".

H 4: The size of the "physical distance" is positively related to the amount of "location planning".

H 5: The amount of "location planning" is positively related to the "performance" i.e. the greater the amount of location planning the higher the probability of success, and the smaller the amount of location planning the higher the probability of failure.

The variables and the hypotheses are illustrated in the figure below.

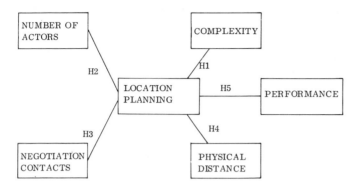

Figure 3:1 The basic model

A number of other relationships also exists, but only these five will be examined.

Two specific characteristics of this basic model, the time dimension and the systems level, will be examined before starting to build the "extended model".

3.4   Some Characteristics of the Model

In this section two basically methodological issues will be discussed: the time dimension and the systems concept.

The fifth hypothesis, relating location planning to performance, concerns two time periods: before and after the time of the location decision. The purpose of this is to provide a rough validation of the location planning. Theoretically such a validation could have been made in at least two other ways. One way would be to compare the real decision-making process with an a priori standardized process (i.e. a normative process) and the other way would be to compare the chosen geographical site with an optimal site according to a normative location model.

Because of the lack of generally accepted knowledge about the behaviour preceding a site selection (the experience from the six cases being far too insufficient) reliable normative processes do not exist. Nor is it (for practical reasons) possible to select permanently optimal geographical sites. Price relations between factors or production change over time, and this affects the geographical optimality. Also the very choice itself may change the price relations upon which it was based.

The measurement of performance "before and after" is an important part of my methodology. No similar method seems to have been employed in the studies of location problems. In other areas however, predominantly investment studies, this "before and after" methodology is not unusual, especially for studies of innovation.

In such studies a number of different predictions are generally related to success or to failure. In the SAPPHO-study (1971) 122 variables were identified and related to success or failure (29 of each) of paired industrial innovations. See also Sandkull (1970) regarding the case of new products.

In another study the character of a firm's "formal planning system" is related to the success of the subsequent acquisition. This study, which is described by Ansoff et al (1971) involved three tests. One of them shows a strong correlation between individual planning attributes and improvement in performance expressed in sales growth, earning/share, total assets growth and several other measurements. These "objective" financial measurements of the results display a substantial difference between "planners" and "non planners". A subjective evaluation of the results by management, on the other hand, does not show a great difference between planners and non planners. However, managers of firms which planned, claimed on average a lower incidence of failure.

> There appear to be two explanations why perceived achievements show little difference between planners and non planners. First, the firms that did not plan had no explicit statements of expectations and, hence, could more readily adjust their aspirations ex post facto. Secondly, a number of non-planning firms (particularly those seeking vertical acquisitions) achieved success without careful planning and analysis, because their acquisitions were relatively small firms whose operations were already well known to them through previously existing supplier or customer relationships.
> (Ansoff, 1970, p. 4)

These explanations will later prove relevant to my field work.

The following four points in time constitute a formalization of the previous discussion. The location planning takes place between t_1 (=awareness of location problem) and t_2 (=formal selection of site). At t_3 the production at the new site starts and at t_4 the running-in period is completed. Between t_1 and t_2 a further vital point of time can be added, t_{ss} (=starting the search for a site).

Since this study involves the totality of the location choice situation –
i.e. a systems view – the systems concept will be briefly commented.

Systems theory can be regarded as a language useful for describing
simple biological organisms, people, ecological systems, families and
other small groups and even very complicated organized systems, such
as local/regional labour markets or nations. The strength of the
"theory" is that it contributes to increased knowledge of such systems by
relating it to other systems. It has proved especially suitable when
studying hierarchies of systems, since each level acts as the environment of the level beneath it.

In this study three hierarchical system levels will be identified:

1. The <u>location management system</u> includes the people – actors –
    who are involved in the location decision-making. This system
    constitutes a sub-system of

2. The <u>company system</u> which includes everybody within the firm.
    This system is a sub-system of

3. The <u>environment system</u> that includes everything relevant outside
    the company.

The levels are summarized in the figure below:

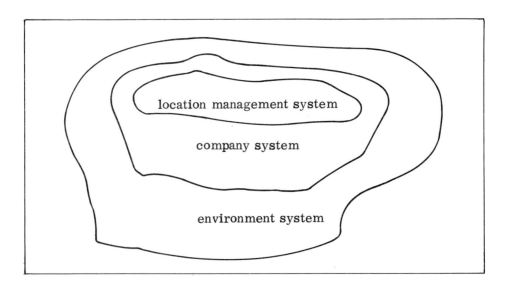

All the six main variables in the basic model belong to the "location management system".

This systems concept will prove important when the extended model is presented and, in particular, when the factors are introduced. In addition, the final chapter of this study will introduce some normative statements which can also be classified using these three levels.

The remainder of this chapter will be devoted to the presentation of an extended model which will later be used to provide the basis for a larger field study. In the next six sections an attempt is made to answer the following three questions:

What relevance have the variables which have been introduced?

What other methods of measuring these variables exist?

What factors influence the values of the variables?

The answers to these questions are primarily based on the case-studies, but a wide range of existing theories and empirical observations are also used.

3.5 Location Planning

There are four closely related, but distinct, ways of defining this variable. Throughout the remainder of the study these will be identified as "A", "B", "C" and "D". While each of these definitions is relevant in particular circumstances, the first one "A", is of primary importance to this study.

A: The "source" definition

Location planning is defined as the number of sources used - i.e. the number of publications, models and techniques and people consulted - during the site selection process. The following table illustrates this definition using material drawn from the case studies.

Publications	Models and techniques	People who were consulted
Secondary data such as county plans (läns-planer), file of documentation from the Federation of Swedish Industries and the Ministry of Labour and Housing (Industriför-bundets och Inrikesde-partementets pärm), publications from "Lokaliseringsbyrån" etc.	Investment calculus, discounted cash-flow, location models etc.	Discussions with other firms on potential sites, the County Employment Board Director (läns-arbetsdirektören) etc.

B: The "model of systematic behaviour" definition

Location planning is defined by the extent to which actual behaviour corresponds with an a priori model of systematic behaviour. The model is inspired by a "scenario of righteous behaviour" also called an a priori pattern of "good management" presented by Townroe in 1972 (pp. 262-263). The model of this study consists of the following six questions:

1. Were the requirements written down?

2. Was the list of alternative sites drawn up in a systematic manner?

3. Was the evaluation of sites systematic?

4. Did the arguments concern the future when evaluating the sites?

5. Were the evaluations based on explicit cost estimations?

6. Were more than two alternatives evaluated?

Affirmative answers to these questions are identified as systematic behaviour.

C: The "cost" definition

Location planning is defined by the amount of money spent on the preparation of the location decision. The well-known decision rule in economics, to produce until MR=MC, can be transferred to search situations. This merely states the economic fact that it costs money to investigate alternatives. The manager will go on searching for further location sites until additional refinements no longer pay for the cost of the search. The experience from these and other cases, however, points to the fact that the amount of resources devoted to search is determined by other factors than a possible refinement, and that the concept of aspiration is very difficult to identify and formulate.

My intention here is to identify cost components and to estimate the size of real costs incurred in collecting the data. The sum should be a valid indicator of the amount of location planning.

The cost aspect is treated by Townroe (1972, p. 270) but he puts the question in a way that neither verifies nor falsifies any of my hypotheses. One of his general hypotheses is: "that the cost of gathering information does not explicitly limit the search".

D: The "time" definition

Finally, location planning is defined by the time which location planning takes, i.e. between t_1 and t_2. A number of researchers such as Simon (1945, pp. 46-47) suggest using the time devoted to a problem as an indicator.

The first factor influencing the variable location planning will now be introduced.

Competition (R 19)

It was only L'Oreal that really commented on the question of competition during my informal interviews. In their case the competition in the cosmetics market was fairly high. I will assume, that the amount of location planning is a function of competition, both on the input and the output side. It is a common assumption in neoclassical economic theory at least, that high competition decreases profit margins and therefore the degree of freedom available when making important decisions. This is equivalent to the assumption: the higher the competition the bigger the amount of location planning. Empirical evidence verifying this proposal is, however, rare.

The relationship between this factor and the variable location planning is shown in the model as follows.

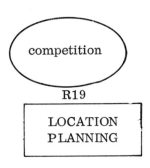

R19

LOCATION
PLANNING

3.6 Complexity

This variable concerns the complexity of the total problem situation and is defined by the number of other decisions involved in addition to the location decision. When this number is large, it is assumed that the attention focused on the location decision is limited, and location planning will therefore be small.

The role of the location decision – its order among other decisions, the interdependence between it and other decisions and the influence of every other decision on the location selection – has been studied on a case-study basis (see section 1.6) but not in a wider context through inter-firm comparisons. Nor do any formalized measures to describe this interdependence seem to have been developed. One conclusion from these studies is, however, that the treatment of the location decision is probably not as thorough in a domestic context as in cases where foreign plant investments are considered.

One factor which is assumed to influence the complexity variable is discussed below.

Cause for and steps taken before the location planning (R 6)

It is an assumption of this study that the degree of complexity depends among other things on the efforts made to avoid a move before the location planning starts i.e. before the time for awareness t_1. This may mean that one or more of the seven other decisions, apart from the location decision, is taken in advance. This assumption (factor) is supported by data from the six cases. For example, Sandviken and Fagersta made their market decisions long before anybody was aware of any location problems. The relationship between this factor and the complexity variable is shown in the following model.

69

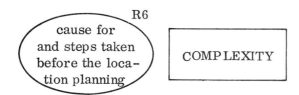

cause for
and steps taken
before the loca-
tion planning

R6

COMPLEXITY

3.7 Number of Actors

This section will examine the relevance of the variable "number of
actors" and its relationship to the amount of location planning. Reference will be made to theories based on a number of studies.

First a study by Downs (1971, p. 78) supports my hypothesis (H 2).
This study concludes that to "restrict decision making to a small number" is the kind of "policy" that tends "to contract degree of search
and narrow diversity of alternatives considered".

The number of participants or actors in a process is related to the
management style prevailing. The concept of style, however, does
not have any generally accepted definition, although an open style is
normally assumed to imply the involvement of many actors and a closed
style the involvement of only a few. Two well-known classifications are
the dichotomies: centralization - decentralization (in traditional organization theory) and mechanistic - organic (Burns & Stalker, 1961). These
pairs of concepts have usually been thought of as synonymous. However,
a recent work ("Designing Complex Organisations": Galbraith, 1973)
suggests that in the case of "decentralized" and "organic" this is not so.

Recent empirical results show that highly centralized decisions, involving few actors, tend to be bad decisions. This is shown in a study
by Rockley (1969, p. 236) who investigated 69 English firms in great
detail. These conclusions may be interpreted as a location situation
where "few actors" lead to a small amount of location planning and
later to a "bad performance". Thus two of my hypotheses (H 2 and
H 5) are supported.

Another type of theory concerning the number of actors involved in
making decisions, examines the costs of internal communication. It
is true that decisions made by a lot of people (often called organizational
decision-making) involve costs which are not incurred when only one

actor is involved. For example, errors of transmission or distortion or channels of communication overloaded in the short run lead to a loss of efficiency. And internal communication absorbs resources, particularly time. On the other hand, organizations (i.e. many actors) have certain advantages over "one-actor decision-makers" such as greater capacity and more information for carrying out the decision and action cycle, extensive internal specialization, and the ability to draw on a diversity of viewpoints (see Downs, 1971, p. 71).

A numbers of factors affecting this variable will now be identified and discussed.

Actor´s attitude towards secrecy (R 7)

This is a factor within the location management system that tends to limit the number of actors.

The location problem is a unique problem and will probably give rise to a good deal of rumour and speculation, which can only obstruct the work of those responsible for solving it. A lot of people have an interest in the problem, not only people in the firm, but also those who live near the potential sites. Another aspect which increases the uncertainty is the political environment (subsidies etc) in which the problem has to be solved. Fear of losing workers was the reason why the management of L´Oreal and Oliver did not tell the employees about the plan to move until very late. Townroe (1971, p. 114) says that

> ... the range of possibilities was restricted for 40 % of the firms by the need for secrecy within the company to ensure that only a minimum number of people knew a move was being contemplated.

Yet another argument that highlights the relevance of this factor is that secrecy may enable more complex decisions to be made. If a great many people must be involved in making a decision it becomes difficult to communicate to each person the issues involved, the possible alternatives, and the responses and views of their consultants. But if secrecy restricts the number of people consulted, these people can consider much more complicated possibilities (Downs, 1971, p. 77).

Company characteristics (R 8)

The actors in the location problem-solving group do not act in a vacuum. There is an environment - a company - with structural characteristics that have a great impact on the group. On the company system level it seems reasonable to assume that the bigger the company the bigger the location management group, because of interest pressures from different parts of the company. Probably ownership and goals have an impact on the size of the group as well. For example, in a state-owned company the demands for knowledge about management´s activities are greater and tend to produce a more open management style. One official reason for the state ownership of companies is that is makes it easier to fulfil regional goals when the companies concerned need more capacity and hence new locations. A factor that tends to reduce the size of the location group is prior experience of solving location problems. If the organizational learning is highly developed and a routine approach has been developed, the size of the group might be smaller. On the other hand it could be argued that when no prior knowledge exists, the situation is so complex and uncertain that few would feel capable of participating in it.

The last structural feature concerns the earlier mentioned concept of centralization. In a company strictly centralized and dominated by a managing director or chairman who can essentially make up his own mind without reference to others, the location group is small.

Size of location project (R 9)

Clearly the number of actors involved in the location planning will be affected by the size of the new establishment. (Turnover, number of employees etc.) For example the Sveg establishment was of limited magnitude, while L´Oreal with 1,000 employees was planning to relocate the whole factory.

Conflicts between actors (R 10)

To bring many people into decision-making, especially when those involved have a wide variety of views and interests, will lead to conflicts (March & Simon, 1958, chapter 5 and Cyert & March, 1963).

This conflict factor concerns the location management system. It was not verified in the six cases but has shown up in other empirical works. Loasby reports (1967, p. 42) that twelve interviewers agreed there had been marked differences of opinion amongst those involved in the search for a new site.

Actors´ behaviour (R 11)

The former factor concerned interpersonal conflicts. These conflicts are assumed to be dependent on the behaviour of the actors. Such behaviour is then assumed to be related to a set of the actor´s characteristics.

Certain individual behavioural features might have an impact on the tendency for conflicts to emerge. Do these features represent "impetus" or

72

"status quo" forces? (See Bower, 1970.) Which person initiated the location issue? What is the behaviour during site visits? In Fagersta and Trelleborg the immediate personal relationships between certain actors and local officials were considered decisive by the companies. This rather general factor is thus supposed to influence the degree of "conflicts between actors".

Actors´ background characteristics (R 12)

The "Actors´ background characteristics" affect the "Actors´ behaviour". The relationship between them is designated R 12.

One observation from the cases in chapter 2 is that most key actors are engineers. As there are many business specialists available within the firms, this fact indicates that the location problem is influenced by the actors´ education and that it is usually regarded as a technical problem to be handled by technicians.

A second characteristic affecting the behaviour might be the actors´ familiarity with similar problem situations. Although this seems reasonable, there is little evidence from the six cases to support this view.

The third characteristic concerns the actors´ occupations. Surprisingly, many of the actors belonged to the very top group of managers. In the L´Oreal case there were some assistants involved who might be called planners. Also Kjellman at Trelleborg was a planner.

Recent empirical evidence concerning the importance of this characteristic is outlined in Lorange (1973, p. 13). He divides the people involved in unstructured decision-making into planners (staff oriented) and top management (line or management oriented). The tasks of the former relate to the "substance" of planning and those of the latter to the planning "process". However an efficient manager must focus on both jobs. A conclusion formulated by Lorange (ibid., p. 13) is that

> ... the most effective of the two tasks takes place when the differences are thoroughly recognized and the tasks are separated among the planners so that the different working relationships required with top management can be reflected.

The factors and relations introduced in this section are illustrated below. Two of the factors "size of location project" and "company characteristics" belong to the company system, while the other three are within the location management system.

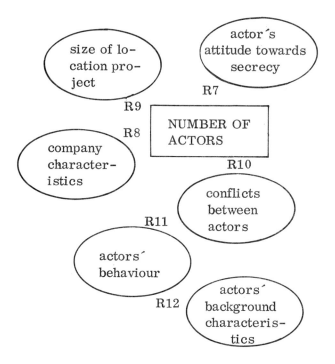

3.8 Negotiation Contacts

This variable concerns the frequency with which various authorities are contacted. The contacts concern negotiations for subsidies of different types. The number of hours is assumed to be negatively related to the amount of the location planning (H 3).

In considering the relevance of this variable, certain relationships between the company system and the environment seem important.

Political processes, that is the influence of participants outside the firm such as Government, are fully recognized in practice (Greiner, 1967, p. 120). The need for more knowledge about such processes, especially concerning large firms, is stressed by Bower (1970, pp. 2-3). Involvement of, or pressures from, outsiders are especially frequent in the decision processes concerning location. Any clear evidence of the role played by these kinds of incentive is very rare. The participation of authorities on different levels is superficially described in some of the earlier quoted case-studies, and in Cameron & Clark (1966).

From some points of view the interdependence between a plant and its environment is great. It is quite clear that location decisions to a great extent affect the individual´s life style since they have a direct bearing upon employment and housing. This fact has made most governments attempt to control or influence future locational patterns through regulations and/or incentives. For past and present regional policies in Sweden, see the report SOU 1974:82. The tools of the Swedish authorities are at present information, grants, loans (see Larsson, 1970) and the use of investment funds (Grundberg, 1972 and Rondén & von Schwerin, 1974). In practice the firms have to apply for most of the subsidies. Besides written applications, bargaining and negotiations are not uncommon features according to the case-studies.

In my terminology I label all those activities aimed at obtaining subsidies "negotiation contacts". My suggestion is that from the firm´s point of view it is principally a question of selecting one of two strategies or "search rules". In the six processes described the strategies are contradictory. They may be called:

1. "The political strategy" i.e. a large amount of "negotiation contacts".

2. "Economic business strategy" i.e. a large amount of "location planning".

Sources of finance (R 13)

The case-studies indicate that interest in incentives varies between firms. Trelleborg and Fagersta, for example, made two kinds of calculations, one including and one excluding subsidies. Firms with ample financial resources do not have to worry so much about subsidies. When arguing for the relevance of this factor on the environment system level, it is necessary to use a very broad view. Therefore I will first comment upon the effects of regional policy, after which I will briefly describe the type of selective policy prevailing in Sweden and, finally, mention some disadvantages of centralized control.

The size of the firm plays an important role here. Of all the inducements mentioned there is one that is closely associated with big firms, namely investment funds. The branches at Bollnäs and Sveg, for example, were financed by the investment fund. In addition the law specifies that either investment funds or the normal locational grants/loans may be used for a particular location project, but not both.

A large number of books and articles have been written about the effects of regional policy. However, the achievements of Swedish regional policy are unclear. There are arguments in favour of the scheme e.g. in SOU 1974:82, where it is pointed out that unemployment in the northern counties of Sweden has decreased. Some say on the other hand that regional policy is a big failure due to, amongst other things, the inefficiency and lack of variety of the instruments (Rhenman, 1975, p. 94). A third type of literature does not evaluate the policy but estimates the costs and the revenues for society e.g. the number of new employees (Wibble, 1973, section V.4).

Regional policy in Sweden is a selective policy. It is a common statement that selective policies favour the big companies that have their own bureaucracies which can establish relationships with the public administration. These relationships increasingly take on the character of negotiations. The large number of small and middle-sized firms cannot maintain a similar personal contact with the state bureaucracy. One thousand leaders of small companies cannot negotiate about individual subsidies and thus only large firms tend to be considered (Lindbeck, 1972, p. 36, Albinsson, 1972, p. 52). This leads to a new coalition not between political parties but between government, civil servants and the leaders of large companies. This phenomenon could be called "myglingsekonomi", where representatives of these categories negotiate advantages for the individual firm.

Over the past few years the selective nature of national policy has become more pronounced (Albinsson, 1972, p. 51). The scope of selectivity has widened and the issue of permits is more and more influenced by individualistic considerations. This not only involves the date for making the investment but also the type of industry, geographical location and type of capital investment. This increase in selectivity is caused by the rising ambitions of the government. Earlier the stabilization policy was directed towards smoothing out large cyclical fluctuations. For this purpose rough general instruments were sufficient. Since the current ambition is to create employment for minor segments of the population, this leads to isolated achievements of different kinds. One danger in this kind of policy is the lack of professionalism. Politicians and bureaucrats undertake tasks for which they lack the qualifications, i.e. to manage companies. A conclusion, of a more speculative character, is that entrepreneurs will progressively learn that it is more profitable to negotiate and obtain special advantages from the authorities than to make attempts to increase the efficiency and competitive ability of their firms (ibid., pp. 51-52). The hypothesis H 3 may be regarded as supporting this speculative conclusion.

There are other problems associated with central "interventions" of
the kind discussed above. Allocation losses can "set in" if the price
system is destroyed. This means that investment and production perhaps will not be attracted to the optimum areas. It is very difficult to
quantify this problem, but it is probably not unimportant. Investment
funds constitute a typical case. In practice only about 15 % of Swedish
industry has access to these funds. Within this group, the funds subsi-
dize 30-40 % of the cost of new buildings and·10-12 % of new machinery.
Firms outside the group receive no subsidies. One likely outcome of
this policy is that established firms, possibly with obsolete products,
will be subsidized at the expense of new companies with new products
(Lindbeck, 1972, pp. 35-36).

The availability of "sources of finance" is assumed to affect the factor
"amount of money received/condition". The relationship between them
is designated R 13.

Amount of money received/condition (R 14)

The amount of money, and the conditions under which it was received,
was different in each case. The Sveg establishment was connected with
a condition made by the Ministry of Finance that the branch should
employ a specific number of people. This factor is assumed to be dependent both on the sources of finance (R 13, above) and on the kind of
actors who negotiate (R 15). It may also be related to the number of
contacts with the authorities. Individual managers must decide whether
such contacts are worthwhile.

Actors who negotiate (R 15)

From the six cases we learn that most of the planning is done by executives. One obvious reason for this is that if the approach to the location problem is the "political strategy", the top management would
be involved in the process from the very beginning. The traditional
normative planning approach however is that planners prepare the
problems, and managers then make the decisions. It would seem reasonable to argue that if a company wishes to receive the maximum subsidy
possible, then it must ensure that the correct actor carries out the negotiations.

Conflicts between authorities (R 16)

A large number of different institutions and officials are concerned
with regional and location problems. In the case of Trelleborg the
attitudes of officials in Östersund proved the relevance of this factor.

In the figure below the variable, the factors introduced and the relationships between them are illustrated. The factor "actors who negotiate"
belongs to the location management system while the rest are environment system concepts.

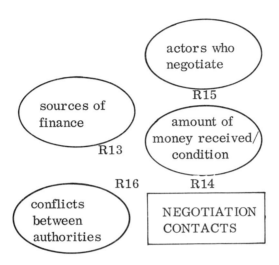

3.9 Physical Distance

Oliver and L´Oreal moved - and Trelleborg was intending to move -
a relatively long distance. These cases also involved a considerable
amount of location planning. The other companies moved a shorter
distance and carried out a smaller amount of location planning. These
were the empirical observations on which hypothesis H 4 was based.
Now some theories will be described which further support the relevance of the distance variable. After this description two factors
affecting this variable will be introduced.

The distance variable frequently occurs in theoretical literature, mostly
in the context of explanations for the development of trade. In the traditional theory of international trade, economic distance was on the whole
ignored. During the sixties, however, with the help from the gravita-
tion and potential models already used in regional sciences (but originating from physics), distance was brought in as an explanatory factor.
Many empirical studies lately have shown the strong explanatory power
of the distance factor. Gruber & Vernon have written "... the distance
factor, D_{ij}, has strong explanatory power for most product classes..."
(1970, p. 260). My initial hypothesis that the greater the distance the
greater the amount of location planning, is related to these theories but
on a micro level.

78

Traditional location theories such as those developed by Weber (1909) and Lösch (1954), are all based on the effect of distance on the cost of transport. These normative theories result in optimal geographical positions for plants. After the Second World War these types of theories have continually been refined and developed by operations researchers. The object function is almost exclusively a question of minimizing the transportation cost.

But the distance factor is a wide concept with different implications. I shall therefore present some different meanings of distance. Johansson (1966) introduces new perspectives on the term "distance" in order to explain certain aspects of the international trade in quality steel. His results show that "cultural closeness or distance" is more important in some cases than the "geographical closeness" for the structure of the international steel trade. Discussing the desirability and possibility of controlling foreign subsidiaries, Ekman (1967) introduces the concept of "environmental gap". Another example is Kindleberger (1962). He stressed that trade is not a matter of geographical distance but of "economic distance".

With regard to the period of diffusion of innovations, a particularly important bias in "interpersonal communication" is that imposed by distance. As Hägerstrand (1953) and others have pointed out, for most people interaction with other individuals is restricted and the probability of contact declines as the distance between individuals increases. This relationship has been termed the neighbourhood effect. Information spreads outwards from the originating source and the likelihood that a particular item will be absorbed decreases as the distance from that source increases. Finally, Hörnell, Vahlne and Wiedersheim-Paul (1973, pp. 101-102) distinguish between "physical and psychological distances". The former includes barriers for products and payment flows e.g. tariffs. The latter concerns problems associated with collecting information about barriers or lack of knowledge about them.

A general feature of all these approaches is that distance is inversely related to knowledge. Distance creates barriers to knowledge. This study´s earlier definition of the "physical distance" variable is similar to that of Gruber & Vernon (1970). These authors emphasize the pervasive strength of this variable. They stress that "physical distance" is a measure that includes not only the effect of transport costs but also the effect of other problems such as limitations on managers´ and planners´ knowledge about sources and markets. I share this view.

In Townroe´s studies one of the conclusions is: "The longer Development Areas moves used fewer sources than the local moves, but used the few more intensively. There was a heavy dependence by these moves on lo-

cal and central government agencies as sources of information"
(Townroe, 1971, p. 114). The first part of this statement contradicts
my fourth hypothesis (H 4), which says that longer moves are related to
more location planning i.e. more sources. It indicates however the need
for a further factor "classification of area in which site is located",
which will be explained below. Townroe also presents another general
hypothesis regarding distance. The "longer the distance of the proposed
move the more consideration is given to not moving at all" (1972, p. 270).
He does not make clear how "more consideration" is measured. But
supposing it is equivalent to a large amount of location planning using
my definition, then this hypothesis will support my hypothesis H 4.

Classification of area in which site is located (R 17)

This factor is a correction factor to physical distance. I intend to distinguish between Development Areas and other areas. The fact that
L'Oreal and Oliver were directed at an early stage towards Development Areas, motivated my selection of this factor. It has sometimes
been suggested that firms intending to move to Development Areas are
to a lesser degree "rational" in their planning behaviour than other
companies planning moves. Townroe's hypothesis that "Development
Area moves consider a smaller number of alternatives than non-De-
velopment Area moves" (1972, p. 270) supports this suggestion. The
study by Cameron & Clark (1966) produced similar results. The proposed relationship between this factor and "physical distance" is referred to as R 17 in the model.

Attitudes to different areas (R 18)

The last variable in this section also constitutes a form of correction
factor to the geographical distance. It was quite obvious in the case-
studies - particularly with Trelleborg - that the actors' attitudes to
regional differences is very crucial. Certain areas were dismissed
as possibilities before any thought was given to a visit. This element
of prejudgement in the decision process is also raised by Townroe
(1971, p. 66) and in particular by Eversley (1965).

There exist a number of definitions of attitudes. In Cook & Selltiz (1964,
p. 36) four types are distinguished. One of them defines attitude as:
"... an underlying disposition which enters, along with other influences,
into the determination of a variety of behaviours towards an object or
class of objects, including statements of beliefs and feelings about the
object and approach - avoidance actions with respect to it". The authors
prefer this position, as I do, firstly because others (e.g. Allport, 1954)
have concluded that observations of regularities in social behaviour
seem to point to the operation of relatively stable underlying dispositions
toward classes of objects e.g. in this case towards location problems

and towards different areas. And secondly, I believe that apparent in-
consistencies in social behaviour may often be understood in terms of
stable underlying dispositions in shifting relations to other influences of
behaviour (Cook & Selltiz, 1964, pp. 36-37). This factor will be illustrated by identifying and extracting statements of attitude from the six
cases.

The two factors and relations introduced in this section are illustrated
below.

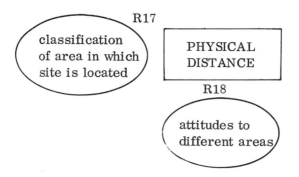

3.10 Performance

The last variable is performance. This is measured at time t_4 (when
the running-in period is completed) and expresses the degree of success
of the location at that time.

Only two of the cases contain judgements of the effectiveness of the
move. In the Bollnäs case, a small amount of location planning was
followed by bad effects - a negative performance. Oliver on the other
hand carried out extensive location planning and the experience afterwards was said to be good.

In the existing literature the evaluation of organizational performance
after a major change seems to be a rare topic. This despite the fact
that there are many methods and models available for project evaluation
(e.g. investment appraisals). Some consumer theories do evaluate individual behaviour, but on the whole the theoretical literature describing
performance after change of any kind is limited, as was pointed out
earlier in section 3.4.

Performance might be dependent on a number of factors. Rapid un-
foreseeable changes in the environment can lead to failure even when
a rigorously prepared location decision has been made. "Adaptive"
behaviour after a "bad" site selection may on the other hand lead to

success. Hypothesis H 5 states that the amount of location planning is positively related to the performance.

It is clearly important to specify the criteria used to measure the performance, since none that are obvious or generally accepted exist. Some multinational firms have developed criteria for the success of their foreign subsidiaries but such general yardsticks appear to be unusual on a national level. My suggestion is therefore to develop multi-objective criteria. That is, to define several dimensions and to conduct a varied appraisal of the effect instead of looking at only one determinant of success or failure.

The following method was used to develop this instrument. I interviewed informally a number of professors in Business Administration at Stockholm University and at the European Institute for Advanced Studies in Management at Brussels. They had all read a thesis proposal preceding this draft and I asked them to suggest performance variables. This resulted in a number of suggestions which were classified as follows:

1. Objective criteria

    Changes in the unit cost due to the change of site.

2. Semi-objective criteria

    The degree to which expectations are met: actual outcomes compared with expected outcomes regarding production volume, turnover, new employees, product line and profitability (productivity). (These two terms are regarded as synonymous in the field research.)

3. Subjective criteria

    Individual assessment (by actors) of the degree of success/failure. For a very practical reason this subjective approach is liable to be biased. The proportion of "successes" will probably be great since most people tend to rationalize their earlier behaviour. This is what Festinger calls "cognitive dissonance" and what Vroom refers to as a way of resolving "post choice dissonance".

    However, three kinds of subjective instruments are used. The first aims at giving a summarized judgement of the success of the location from a geographical point of veiw, the second uses a scoring model and the third measures performance indirectly by simulating the earlier situation of site selection. In fact six different attributes constituting the criteria of performance will be developed. The attributes, which appear in the questionnaire in the next chapter, are labelled in the following manner:

Class of attribute	Refers to the letter:
Objective criteria	B ("change in unit cost") D ("change in unit cost")
Semi-objective criteria	C ("expectations are met")
Subjective criteria	A ("geographical") E ("scoring model") F ("simulating the earlier situation")

Demand (R 20)

Increased demand is sometimes the original motive for starting location planning. This was the reason in the case of Bollnäs, Fagersta
and L´Oreal, and in the case of Oliver a genuine market penetration
preceded the good performance. But what role does the demand situation play for the evaluation of the performance? Does a "boom" explain
a success better than the selection of a well situated site? The factor
"demand" which is located in the environment system, is assumed to be
related to the performance variable. Their relationship is designated
R 20.

3.11   The Extended Model

Before presenting the complete extended model a summary of the
chapter will be made.

Based on the localization processes in chapter 2 six variables: location
planning, complexity, number of actors, negotiation contacts, physical
distance and performance were generated. Five hypotheses about the
relationships between these variables have been postulated. The
variables and the hypotheses constitute the basic model.

One basic function of the model is the study of one period of time
(t_1-t_2) during which the location planning takes place as well as one
point of time (t_4) when performance is measured. Another basic
characteristic is the three system levels: location management system,
company system and environment system. The argument for classification is to create a more elaborate model by devoting each of the identified variables and factors to any system level. Another argument is
later on to make possible a presentation of ordered normative statements.

Based on this model a number of factors affecting different variables
were then identified. There are 15 factors altogether. This is also
the number of proposed relationships. This stage of identification was
mainly based on evidence from and illustrated with examples from the

localization processes. A number of very different theories and other empirical observations have also been used as evidence when constructing the extended model.

The basic purpose of the model-building is to provide a basis for a larger field study. Therefore the extended model will constitute a very important framework for further empirical observations.

The complete model is as follows:

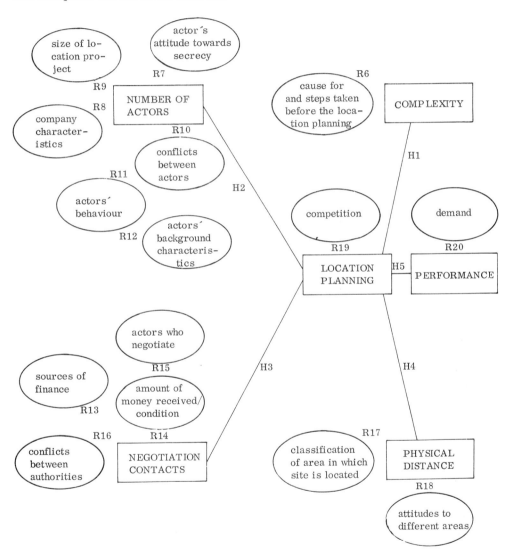

Figure 3:2. The extended model. The core is the basic model including six variables (in the boxes) and five hypotheses (H1 – H5). The remainder consists of 15 factors (in the ovals) that are assumed to affect the variables through 15 relationships (R6–R20).

84

"... Now, if you have a green balloon, they might think you were
only part of the tree, and not notice you, and if you have a blue
balloon, they might think you were only part of the sky, and not
notice you, and the question is: Which is most likely?"
(Winnie-the-Pooh)

CHAPTER 4   METHODS OF DATA COLLECTION

The method of acquiring data for the proposed extended model in
chapter 3 will be explained. A number of successive stages in the
empirical research are then discussed in great detail before the
questionnaire - a formalization of the model - is presented. Finally the method of carrying out the field study is described.

4.1   Selection of Method

It must be remembered that the basic purpose of this study is to describe localization processes. The method chosen to achieve this purpose has been to construct the model that was presented in chapter 3.
The question is whether this "extended model" is a valid representation
of the real situation. To understand its strengths and weaknesses - i.e.
to verify the generality of the variables, factors and relationships - the
rest of the study will be devoted to a confrontation with empirical data.
It is necessary first to collect data since there is no relevant empirical
data available. The fact-finding as such is therefore also important.
This means that in subsequent chapters specific emphasis will be put
on the descriptions of the variables and factors, in addition to the study
of the relationships between them. This chapter will concentrate, however, on the design of a field study to fit the above purpose.

But how can the necessary data be collected? To follow a process either as an observer (see Bower, 1970) or as a participant-observer (like the social anthropologists) is a time-consuming process. Although these are powerful and reliable methods, they are extremely hard on resources; localization processes can span periods of years. The researcher also runs the risk that the location project will be abandoned. For these reasons it was decided to base the whole study on a retrospective approach.

The structure of the extended model implies that not only must a final decision have been made, but a certain amount of time must have elapsed after the move so that performance can be observed and measured.

The disadvantages of location surveys based on postal questionnaires have been mentioned. Two further problems are that a high proportion of questionnaires are simply not answered - a consequence of the complexity of location processes - and the danger of not reaching the right people. If one identifies the person involved - an actor - the crucial point is of course to get him to remember data that sometimes dates back several years, and to induce him to remember real facts. By separately interviewing at least two of the people involved, it should however be possible to reconstruct facts with greater certainty. A very important lesson learned from the field study was the significance of the roles played by the respondents. It is highly desirable to interview actors i.e. those people who had the real power in a selection between sites.

A further experience from the cases is that managers and planners regard this type of problem as secret. It is therefore important to create an atmosphere of confidence. Documents and other written information forming the decision base are rare. One of the advantages of interviewing is that it may provide an opportunity to read this kind of document. With respect to other data-generating mechanisms, laboratory experiments are of limited value when not much is known about the variables and their relationships. Since it is difficult to simulate the "physical distance" of the move and to measure "performance" because of the time lag, this method for data collection was eliminated.

The number of cases is often open to argument when a field study is being designed. Important factors when deciding the number of cases are:

1.   The purpose of the empirical research; to illustrate, to generate or to test hypotheses. The purpose of this field study is threefold:

86

1. To describe the variables and the factors

2. To test the hypotheses

3. To describe the relationships

Of these, a test of hypotheses generally requires a larger number of cases. A secondary purpose may be distinguished: to generate additional hypotheses from the descriptions.

Very often it is necessary to distinguish between clinical unstructured methods and more analytical structured methods (Normann, 1973, p. 51) where, in both cases, a great many variables are measured. My study of six cases was of the clinical unstructured type, and its primary purpose was to generate variables. In the forthcoming empirical research, the orientation will be towards a more analytical structured method, since my purpose is to test and also to generate hypotheses.

2.   The number of variables and factors. When this number is high, the number of cases is generally small and vice versa. Since the extended model from chapter 3 is rather comprehensive, this forms an argument for a limited number of cases.

3.   The possibility of acquiring data. As we have seen, official statistics on these matters are nonexistent or totally unreliable, due to the lack of generally accepted definitions. In the six cases, however, I was greatly helped by the contacts I was able to make through acquaintances. The critical thing was to obtain an informal interview within a company. Therefore my sample of six cases was dictated rather by the opportunity to interview, than by a systematic method of sampling. In all, my experience from this phase of data collection revealed great difficulties in obtaining access to companies, which suggests that a limited number of cases should be adopted.

4.2   Stages in the Empirical Research Work

In light of the above discussion and the definitions suggested, it is now possible to characterize the empirical field study as follows:

- interview
- analytical structured
- historical or genetic type
- limited number of cases

However, a number of questions remain unanswered. The rest of the chapter will be devoted to the following stages of designing the empirical work.

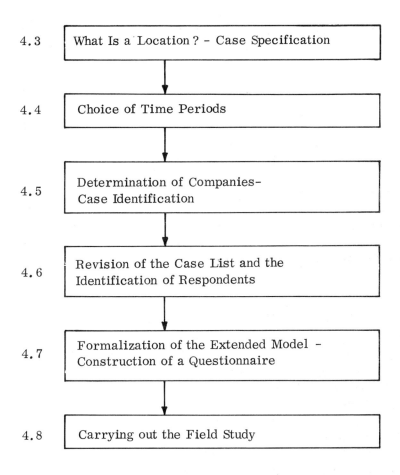

4.3	What Is a Location ? - Case Specification
4.4	Choice of Time Periods
4.5	Determination of Companies- Case Identification
4.6	Revision of the Case List and the Identification of Respondents
4.7	Formalization of the Extended Model - Construction of a Questionnaire
4.8	Carrying out the Field Study

4.3 What Is a Location ? - Case Specification

In chapter 1, I defined the problem to be studied. A number of criteria were introduced. Two of these will be defined more precisely in this section - the type of "new workforce" and the type of "footloose industries".

First, all locations where the "new" workforce is drawn from the same labour pool as the old, are excluded. Frequently production expands and a new and bigger factory is established "across the road", i.e. within the same local labour market. I must, however, allow situations in which some key workers move with the plant. It seems reason-

88

able to set the limit that one year after production start-up more than half the employee stock must have been recruited from the area around the location site.

A further requirement is that the number of employees should not be less than 25 during the year of establishment i.e. 12 months from production start-up. The reason for this is to exclude the smallest firms where it may be assumed that highly personal considerations prevail and that very little, if any, search activity has preceded the move.

Secondly, we can consider the type of industry. Engineering, which constitutes half the manufacturing sector of the Swedish economy, is a suitable example of "footloose" industry. Plants producing goods, at the dates of establishment, belonging to the SNI-code numbers 37 and 38 will form the population.

4.4 Choice of Time Periods

The starting-up of a factory often involves unexpected events and costly measures. This is further developed in a study by Hånell (1972). One of the most experienced companies in locating branches in Sweden is L M Ericsson. They use three years as a rule of thumb running-in period before a desired productivity level is reached. A systematic study covering several locations within Development Areas stresses the running-in difficulties, as well as their variations between factories. But in general they were said to have ended two years after the date of establishment (Jobin, 1973, p. 14).

The risk that important details might have been forgotten prompted me to use this two-year period as a maximum. This means that if the effects, i.e. performance, were measured during 1974 and the running-in period takes two years, then the latest date for production start-up in the cases considered in this study is late 1971.

4.5 Determination of Companies - Case Identification

Since no official statistical data exist on located companies with the requirements introduced above, other sources must be employed. To get a rough idea of the number of cases, I made an investigation at the National Central Bureau of Statistics (Statistiska Centralbyrån, SCB) in Stockholm. By going through their computer data lists in late 1973 (but without the right to copy the names of the companies) I identified the following yearly distribution of firms fulfilling the above mentioned requirements.

1965	-	27 cases
1966	-	23 "
1967	-	25 "
1968	-	26 "
1969	-	23 "
1970	-	19 "
1971	-	2 "

Since there is no obligation for newly established forms to report to the National Central Bureau of Statistics (Statistiska Centralbyrån, SCB), there is a time lag before the plant is included in the statistics. The data for 1971 and probably for 1970 are wrong, and these statistics are therefore unreliable.

It was the opinion not only of myself but also of some experts from the Federation of Swedish Industries (Industriförbundet), that the reliability of these statistics was not high enough to form the basis for a relatively large field study. Apart from the data being incomplete, there are also coding errors etc.

Having investigated different approaches to identifying the relevant population (public investigations, newspapers etc) I decided that the only feasible way appeared to be direct contact with regional authorities of different kinds. Similar difficulties in identifying companies due to lack of statistics was also a prevailing feature for Rydén (1971), who studied acquisitions and mergers in Sweden.

In January-February 1974, three categories of administrative units in every county were contacted:

1. Head of the Regional Economic Division of the County Board (byråchefen vid regionalekonomiska enheten vid länsstyrelsen)

2. County Employment Board Director (länsarbetsdirektören vid länsarbetsnämnden)

3. Director of Trade Development Association (chefen för företagareföreningen)

I wrote to each of these people in each of 24 counties explaining my research and asking them to give me the name and address of all locations in their particular county with the required properties. Then I telephoned them all to collect their replies. Roughly 25 % of the replies were confirmed by letter. There was a considerable variation in the

quality of the information received. Altogether 47 locations were iden-
tifed by the respondents and these are listed in the table below. Later,
one of the firms proved to have made one more location which also ful-
filled my requirements. This brought the total number of cases to 48.

All the respondents agreed that these three categories of administrative
unit represented the best available sources of information.

Despite this, the information on new locations showed great variations
in accuracy. This conclusion supports the findings of Nygren (1972)
and Levin (1974). The main conclusion is therefore that it must be
nearly impossible for the Government to estimate the effects of their
regional policy when the statistics concerning the locations are so in-
accurate.

A complete list of cases including abbreviated answers from this combined telephone-letter study, shows how great is the need for generally
accepted definitions of locations on which proper statistics could be
based. Further, a list of the names of the places of establishment
shows the pattern of moves and locations in one branch of industry in
Sweden during this two-year period.

| Case no. | County | Source | | | Place of establishment | Relevant case? If not, reasons |
		County Board	County Empl. Board	Trade Dev. Ass.		
1	AB	X			Bandhagen	No. This company, which belongs to a county, has existed since before 1966. In 1970 it was simply placed under a different authority.
2	AB	X			Sundbyberg	No. A move within the municipality. Nearly all the workforce (60) moved with the plant.
3	AB	X			Järna	No. In 1970 the company was legally started when it took over plant, equipment and workforce from another firm.
4	AB	X			Stockholm	No. Just legally started, no production at all.
5	AB	X			Stockholm	No. In 1968 a man from Stockholm bought a company at Motala. Production never moved, it was only controlled from Stockholm.
6	AB	X			Lidingö	No. In 1970 the company moved with all its employees to a new building within the same municipality.

		Source				
Case no.	County	County Board	County Empl. Board	Trade Dev. Ass.	Place of establishment	Relevant case? If not, reasons
7	AB	X			Järfälla	No. In 1969 the company moved with all its employees from Stockholm to Järfälla.
8	AB	X			Västerhaninge	No. Production started 1968/69 in a new building.
9	AB	X			Märsta	No. In 1970/71 the company simply changed its name.
10	C	X	X	X	Tierp	Yes.
11	E	X		X	Kisa	No. Production started in 1968.
12	F			X	Eksjö	No. Only a smaller addition to the building.
13	F			X	Marieholm	No. The company started production of sailing boats in 1973.
14	F			X	Tranås	No. The company moved from Värnamo to Tranås in 1972.
15	G	X		X	Torps Bruk	Yes.
16	H	X	X	X	Oskarshamn	Yes.

Case no.	County	Source County Board	County Empl. Board	Trade Dev. Ass.	Place of establishment	Relevant case? If not, reasons
17	H	X			Västervik	No. The company's branch in Västervik only manufactured plastic boats.
18	I	X		X	Hemse	Yes.
19	K	X		X	Sölvesborg	No. Production started in 1973.
20	K	X		X	Karlskrona	Yes.
21	K	X		X	Ronneby	No. In 1967/68 a plant moved from Södertälje to Ronneby. In 1970/71 a new part-owner was the only change.
22	M	X			Malmö	No. Production started in 1969.
23	N	X	X	X	Halmstad	Yes.
24	P		X		Tranemo	Yes.
25	P	X	X		Borås	Yes.
26	P	X	X		Färjelanda	Yes.
27	R	X		X	Lidköping	Yes.
28	S	X			Arvika	Yes.

		Source				
Case no.	County	County Board	County Empl. Board	Trade Dev. Ass.	Place of establishment	Relevant case? If not, reasons
29	T	X			Kårberg	No. Production started in 1958.
30	U	X		X	Västerås	No. Two machine manufacturers merged.
31	U	X		X	Sala	Yes.
32	W			X	Smedjebacken	Yes.
33	W			X	Mora	Yes.
34	W		X	X	Falun	Yes.
35	W				Ludvika	Yes. Identified by the company through another case on this list.
36	X	X	X		Söderhamn	Yes.
37	Y	X	X	X	Kramfors	Yes.
38	Z	X	X	X	Hede	Yes.
39	Z	X		X	Gällö	Yes.
40	Z	X	X		Sveg	Yes.
41	Z	X	X		Östersund	Yes.
42	Z	X		X	Gällö	No. Production started in 1972.

Case no.	County	County Board	County Empl. Board	Trade Dev. Ass.	Place of establishment	Relevant case? If not, reasons
43	AC			X	Lövånger	No. In 1970 the company changed owner and in 1972 a new plant was inaugurated.
44	AC	X	X	X	Vilhelmina	Yes.
45	BD	X		X	Kalix	Yes.
46	BD	X		X	Piteå	Yes.
47	BD	X		X	Öjebyn	No. Production started in 1972.
48	BD	X		X	Piteå	Yes.

4.6 Revision of the Case List and the Identification of Respondents

In the search for key actors the list was shown to two directors of the Federation of Swedish Industries (Industriförbundet) with long experience of location problems, and to two people at the Swedish Export Council (Exportrådet). These four people with a wide knowledge of Swedish industry, mentioned people to contact in most of the 48 companies on the list.

Existing official data concerning these cases was also investigated in a study by Mikaelsson & Winberg (1974). They classified different location situations starting from the names of the 46 companies identified at that time. By reading:

1. directories: "Handelskalendern", "Kompass", "Vem äger vad i Sverige?", "Svenska aktiebolag", "Svensk Industrikalender"

2. annual reports

and by contacting:

3. Register of Joint Stock Companies

4. National Labour Market Board (Arbetsmarknadsstyrelsen, AMS)

5. all the relevant local authorities

a total of 22 cases were eliminated. The major conclusion was, however, that there were variations in the data provided by the different sources (ibid., p. 16).

The second conclusion derived from this, was that the firms must be contacted directly to find out whether they should belong to the population or not. It must also be added that during the stage of company identification (the telephone/letter study), I came into contact with many civil servants who had worked with loan applications from the firms, given advice to firms regarding possible sites etc. This helped me a lot in my attempts to learn about the search activities and especially the actors in the firms.

When the critical stage in the study arrived, i.e. to contact the company directly, I had already identified one principal participant or knew the name of the managing director in nearly all cases. In March–May 1974 all the companies on the original list (including 48 cases) were contacted by telephone. A large number were eliminated, for different reasons (in the right hand column in the table above the result is presented), which did not surprise me after the study by Mikaelsson & Winberg (1974). However the conclusions from this study and from my telephone/letter investigation were to some extent incongruous. 26 cases remained. These made up the population and I decided to interview all of them. The cases eliminated were not identical with those eliminated by Mikaelsson & Winberg in their study.

Some reflexions must be made on the basis of the revised list:

1. No locations have occurred in any of the three biggest Swedish cities.

2. Of the ten locations suggested in these three cities, none was relevant. The statistics are obviously poorly developed in these three metropolitan counties.

3. The number of eliminated cases is much smaller in Norrland. The congruence between the three sources is greater as well.

The identification of the key actors - the people within the firm who had been most involved in the location process - formed the next step in the empirical work. This work was to a great extent carried out at the same time as the collection of data for the cases. This was very time-consuming since many firms are very big and the key actors had changed their jobs.

As soon as I had established telephone contact with a principal actor or, in some cases, as good a substitute as possible, I asked for an appointment to interview him. As a preparation for the interview a letter was sent explaining the research and enclosing some references (Swedish versions of these are available on request).

4.7 Formalization of the Extended Model - Construction of a Questionnaire

Besides the variables many of the factors introduced in the extended model in chapter 3 have a clear operationalized character. But some other factors are formulated in a way that gives no obvious indication of the nature of the measurements.

In the table below each variable is summarized under a heading called "Nature of variable/factor". The principle of measurement is then described in "Nature of measurement" and the precise question in the column to the right "Question". Some of these principles or instruments are of a "two or three step" type.

Since the field research has the character of fact-finding, the questionnaire is of great importance. A further motive to include the entire questionnaire in the chapter (and not in an appendix) is the fact that the questions are of a combination type. This means here that the questionnaire not only includes questions but also presents methods of interpreting the answers.

Name of variable/ factor	Nature of variable/ factor	Nature of measure-ment	Question (Q)
COMPLEXITY	The scope of complexity of the location choice situation	The number of partial decisions undecided when the search for a site starts at t_{ss}	1. When was the final decision taken concerning choice of product, market, capacity, production technique, date for production start-up, to build or not to build and type of location.

date for final decision

	before t_1	$t_1 - t_{ss}$	$t_{ss} - t_2$	after t_2
product				
capacity				
production technique				
date for production start				
to build or not to build				
kind of location				

Number of final decisions not taken before t_{ss}:

Name of variable/ factor	Nature of variable/ factor	Nature of measure-ment	Question (Q)
Cause for and steps taken before the location planning	1) The scope of reasons initiating location planning	Open question	2. What was the basic cause for considering a new location?
	2) Extent to which other alternatives were considered	Open	3. What alternatives to a new location were discussed?
		Open	4. What steps were taken to avoid moving to a new location by the management, the employees, the local authority or by somebody else?
NUMBER OF ACTORS	Extent to which the management style is open	The total number of people in-volved	5. Which people within the company were involved in the planning (planning includes all activities that occurred between the time when the question of location arose (t_1) to the time of the formal selection of site (t_2))?

Name of variable/ factor	Nature of variable/ factor	Nature of measure-ment	Question (Q)
Actor's attitude towards secrecy	Extent to which the respondent regards the location prob-lem as secret	5-point item	6. To what extent was it important to keep the location planning secret? highly secret — not secret at all
Company charac-teristics	1) Size of the the company	The number of employees	7. How many employees did the com-pany (using the Swedish legal defi-nition) have when the site selection was done?
		The turnover	8. What was the turnover of the com-pany?
	2) Ownership	Classify	9. How was the company's ownership classified at the time of production start-up? - private, not quoted on the stock market - private, quoted on the stock market - publicly owned - cooperative - managing director is the dominant owner - other
	3) Goals	Classify	10. What was the overall goal or policy of the company at the time of the location planning? Rank: profit, growth, self-finance, return on capital, provision of stable employ-ment.
	4) The organi-zation's ex-perience from other location problems	The number of new plants	11. How many plants has the company started in Sweden from 1960 to the the date of this particular site selection?
	5) Extent to which the company is centralized	5-point item	12. How would you describe decision-making in the company according to the following scale? very centralized — very decen-tralized

Name of variable/ factor	Nature of variable/ factor	Nature of measure- ment	Question (Q)
Size of location project	Size of the location	1) The number of em- ployees	How many people were employed at the new location 13. at the production start, 14. after one year, 15. after two years, 16. after three years ?
		2) The turn- over	What was the turnover 17. after one year, 18. after two years, 19. after three years ?
Conflicts between actors	Scope of con- flicts occur- ring between actors during the location planning	Open	20. What types of disparity of views oc- curred during the location planning ?
		Open	21. Describe each of these; at what stage did it occur ?; which actors did it involve ?
		Open	22. How were these differences resolved ?
Actors´ behaviour	1) Extent to which ini- tial aware- ness of the location prob- lem plays a role	Classify	23. Who mentioned the question of loca- tion for the first time ? - an actor - a non-actor - "it just evolved"
	2) Identifica- tion of forces of change	Classify	24. Which people provided impetus or acted as change forces in the location discussions ? - actors - non-actors in the company - non-actors outside the company
	3) Identifica- tion of status quo forces	Classify	25. Which people constituted the status quo forces in the location discussions ? - actors - non-actors in the company - non-actors outside the company
	4) Identifica- tion of pat- terns in visiting be- haviour	Open	26., 27., 28. What location alternatives (specific sites or buildings) were visited and by which actors ? Describe also the order in time when these alternatives were visited and finally the number of working days devoted to each alternative.

Name of variable/ factor	Nature of variable/ factor	Nature of measure-ment	Question (Q)
Actors' background characte-ristics	1) Distribution of occupa-tions	Classify	29. Describe each actor's occupation. Is he - managing director - chairman of the board - production manager - financial manager - investment manager - administrative manager - personnel manager - longe range (strategic) planner - outside consultant - location planner - others ?
	2) Distribution	Classify	30. Is he primarily a manager or a planner ?
	2) Distribution of education	Classify	31. Describe each actor's education. Is he - economist - technician - architect - engineer - accountant - lawyer - sociologist - other education - no formal education
	3) Extent to which each actor is fa-miliar with the problem situation	Open	32. Describe each actor's experience of location problem solving and the num-ber of months that he has devoted to such problems.
	4) Extent to which each actor is ex-perienced in ill-structured problem-solving	Open	33. Describe each actor's experience from other types of problems such as R & D, new products, long-range planning, new technology, etc.

102

Name of variable/ factor	Nature of variable/ factor	Nature of measure-ment	Question (Q)
NETOTIA-TION CONTACTS	Extent to which the company in its location planning is oriented towards nego-tiations for subsidies	1) The number 2) The number	34. How many direct face-to-face nego-tiations took place and how long did they last? 35. How many negotiations took place by telehpone and letters (time for filling in applications etc) and how long did this work take?
Sources of finance	Extent to which differ-ent sources of finance are available	The percentage distribution	36. How was the new plant financed (site + building)? - internal means % - mother company group % - bank % - subsidies % - other %
Amount of money re-ceived/ condition	Extent to which money is received and extent to which condi-tions are imposed	Amount of money and kind of con-dition	37., 38., 39. What types of subsidies and what amounts were received and what conditions were attached to these subsidies?
Actors who negotiate	Extent to which some specific actors are involved in negotiations	Open	40. Which actors negotiatied with which authority about the new location?
Conflicts between authorities	Extent to which autho-rities have conflicting views	Open	41. Did there exist any signs of con-flicts between authorities regarding the size of the subsidies or the con-ditions e.g. priorities of potential location alternatives?
PHYSICAL DISTANCE	Extent to which the new location site is "known"	Number of kilometres	42. (No question asked. The information is taken from a map.)
Classification of area in which site is located	Kind of area	Classify	43. (No question asked. Development Area or not?)

Name of variable/ factor	Nature of variable/ factor	Nature of measure-ment	Question (Q)
Attitudes to different areas	If many res-pondents are interviewed in the same company, the attitudes of the main actors are registered. The differences refer to the new location. and map the attitudes held at the time of the location planning	5-point item	44. The difference between various places in Sweden are generally very big · big · medium · small · no differ-ence at all ∟____∣____∣____∣____⌐
		- " -	45. The difference between a place within the Development Area and a place out-side is generally ∟____∣____∣____∣____⌐
		- " -	46. The difference between a place within a "big town area" (Stockholm, Gothen-burg and Malmö) and a place else-where is generally ∟____∣____∣____∣____⌐
	1) Extent to which spe-cific regions and the size of these are favoured	- " -	47. The difference between a place in Norrland and a place elsewhere in the country is generally ∟____∣____∣____∣____⌐
		- " -	48. The difference between a place in Svealand and a place elsewhere is generally ∟____∣____∣____∣____⌐
		- " -	49. The difference between a place in Götaland and a place elsewhere is generally ∟____∣____∣____∣____⌐
		- " -	50. The differences between sites within various counties are generally ∟____∣____∣____∣____⌐
		- " -	51. The differences between sites within various municipalities are generally ∟____∣____∣____∣____⌐

Name variable/ factor	Nature of variable/ factor	Nature of measure-ment	Question (Q)
	2) Extent to which some specific ar-guments are attached to regional attitudes	5-point item	52. Small places are avoided because the social responsibility can be too big and the future flexibility of the plant therefore reduced. agree completely do not agree at all ⌞___⌟___⌟___⌟___⌟
		- " -	53. Some places are avoided because the prevailing industrial tradition is limited. ⌞___⌟___⌟___⌟___⌟
		- " -	54. Big places are preferred because the potential labour supply is bigger, despite the fact the labour mobility often is higher. ⌞___⌟___⌟___⌟___⌟
		- " -	55. You would decide to locate a plant in an isolated place in order to be alone in the place and therefore not have to compete for labour. ⌞___⌟___⌟___⌟___⌟
		- " -	56. Certain places are avoided because the prevailing attitude there towards industry in general is negative. ⌞___⌟___⌟___⌟___⌟

LOCATION
PLANNING

Name variable/ factor	Nature of variable/ factor	Nature of measure-ment	Question (Q)

The "source" definition (A)	Extent to which "pieces of data" iden-tified in the six location cases are used	The number of "pieces of data" all with the same weight (the total is 27)	57. Which of the following sources were used for the decision base during the the location planning
			
			1) Publication Yes/no
			
			   - county plans (länsplaner)
			   - file of documentation from the Federation of Swedish Industries and the Ministry of Labour and Housing (Industri-förbundets och Inrikes-departementets pärm)

105

Name of variable/ factor	Nature of variable/ factor	Nature of measure-ment	Question (Q)
			Yes/no

2) Models and techniques

- other documentation from the Federation of Swedish Industries or "Industrins loka-liseringstjänst"
- publications from "Lokaliseringsbyrån"
- brochures from local authorities
- brochures from towns
- other advertisements

2) Models and techniques

- index formulas
- estimation of expected value
- point models
- pay-off models
- estimation of return on capital
- discounted cash-flow
- transport models
- location models

3) People who were con-sulted (neither paid nor negotiated with)

- business friend
- banker
- accountant
- manager in other com-pany that has located in potential area
- Trade Development Association (företagarförening)
- Fund for Northern Sweden (Norrlandsfonden)
- County Employment Board Director (länsarbetsdirektör)
- Governor (landshövding)
- County Board

Name of variable/ factor	Nature of variable/ factor	Nature of measure-ment	Question (Q)
			Yes/no
			Officials from the local authorities concerning:
			- the municipality´s plans for the area - the speed of implementing these plans - the political situation
			Number of yes
The "model of systematic behaviour" definition (B)	Extent to which actual behaviour corresponds with an a priori model of systematic behaviour	Open	58. Describe the process of evaluating each alternative. How long did it take? Who started it? Who was the evaluator? What arguments were used?
		Open	59. How were the alternatives compared and evaluated?
		Open	60. What requirements were formulated before the search for location alternatives started?
		Open	61. Which of these were written down? The answers to the questions above were then interpreted subjectively by me in the following "model of systematic behaviour"
			Yes/no
		Number of yes all with the same weight (the total is 6) Classify	1) Were the requirements written down? 2) Was the list of alternative sites drawn up in a systematic manner? 3) Was the evaluation systematic? 4) Did the arguments concern the future when evaluating the sites? 5) Were the evaluations based on explicit cost estimations? 6) Were more than two alternatives evaluated?
			62. Number of yes

Name of variable/factor	Nature of variable/factor	Nature of measurement	Question (Q)
The "cost" definition (C)		The amount of money	63. What did the location planning cost, including data collection and negotiation?
			64. Was any cost limit (project budget etc) concerning the search for location alternatives determined before the search started? Yes/no
		Date	65. If yes, when?
The "time" definition (D)	The time period during which somebody has been aware of the location problem	The time in months	66. At what time was the location alternative mentioned for the first time?
		- " -	67. When did the question of location appear for the first time on an agenda-paper?
		- " -	68. When was the formal site selection done?
		- " -	69. When did the production start (month/year) at the new location?
		Classify	70. Were any time limits for the search established before it started? Yes/no
		Date	71. If yes, when?
		5-point item	72. How strong was the necessity to find a new site?

absolutely necessary .... not necessary at all

Competition	Extent to which competition was experienced	- " -	73. Did the company experience pressure of competition on the product market during the location planning?

very strong .... very weak

		- " -	74. ... on the labour market ...

Name of variable/ factor	Nature of variable/ factor	Nature of measure-ment	Question (Q)
		5-point item	75. ... on other resource markets ... L____|____|____|____⌐
Demand	The relative demand per-ceived by the respon-dent	– " –	The average inflow of orders was from 76. the time of awareness until the time of the interview very very large small L____|____|____|____⌐
		– " –	77. the time of awareness until the time of formal site selection (=location planning) L____|____|____|____⌐
		– " –	78. the time of formal site selection un-til the production start L____|____|____|____⌐
		– " –	79. the production start until the time of the interview L____|____|____|____⌐
PERFORM-ANCE			
l) Objective criteria	Change in unit cost (B, D)	– " –	80. The present average unit cost, com-pared with that at the time of site selection (in fixed prices) is: much much bigger less L____|____|____|____⌐
		– " –	81. The actual average unit cost, com-pared with the amount estimated at the time of site selection (in fixed prices) was: L____|____|____|____⌐

Name of variable/factor	Nature of variable/factor	Nature of measurement	Question (Q)
		Express this cost in percent and suppose actual average cost at t_2 is 100%	82. What was the estimated average unit cost for the principal product in the new plant expected to be after the running-in period, according to the estimations that were conducted at the time of the formal site selection (in fixed cost)?
		- " -	83. What was the average unit cost after the running-in period?
2) Semi-ojective criteria	Degree to which expectations are met (C)	5-point item	84. The actual production volume compared with that expected was: much bigger much less L_____I_____I_____I_____⌐
		- " -	85. The actual turnover compared with that expected was: L_____I_____I_____I_____⌐
		- " -	86. The actual number of new employees (new jobs) compared with that expected was: L_____I_____I_____I_____⌐
		- " -	87. The actual profitability (productivity) compared with that expected was: L_____I_____I_____I_____⌐
		- " -	88. The actual change in the product line during the running-in period compared with that expected was: L_____I_____I_____I_____⌐
3) Subjective criteria	Extent to which success/failure is perceived (A)	l) 5-point item	89. Was the plant, after the running-in period and purely from a geographical point of view, with a summarized judgment: very successful as expected very unsuccessful L_____I_____I_____I_____⌐

Name of variable/ factor	Nature of variable/ factor	Nature of measure-ment	Question (Q)
	Extent to which success/ failure is per-ceived (E)	2) Construc-tion of a scoring model	90. Which factors do you consider when judging whether the location has been successful or not?
			91. List and rank the four most impor-tant
			92. Estimate each factor along a 5-point scale with the background of the new location
		The ranking order gives weights to the factors:	

weight/factor	5-point scale				
	1	2	3	4	5

93. Calculate the <u>total sum:</u>

	Extent to which success/ failure is perceived (F)	Indirect way of measure-ment Classify	94. If you were to make the same location decision today, would you select the same place? Yes/no

111

The order of the questions in the final questionnaire followed my estimation of the extent to which the individual question was sensitive: I
started with more simple, less controversial question areas and progressively went on to more difficult and more value-oriented questions.
The order of the questions in the last section was mainly based on the
presentation of variables and factors in chapter 3.

Instead of using a tape recorder, I brought an assistant to each interview. These people - I employed altogether five post-graduate stu-
dents - wrote protocols from the interviews. The interviews thus gave
a lot more information than the questionnaire. This arrangement en-
abled me to concentrate wholly on the respondent.

The first interview was conducted in March 1974 and was the only one
that month. The rest of the interviews were conducted in May, June,
July and August. The length of the interviews varied from two to five
hours. The average time was three hours. I estimate that it took,
on average, four to five hours to complete a questionnaire. All questions involving five-point answers were written down and handed to the
respondent during the interview in order to clarify the question. Immediately after the interview my assistant and I went through the questionnaire. We discussed and agreed upon the answers to the more subjective
questions.

A surprisingly high proportion of the actors were from the top management of the companies. It was sometimes difficult to agree on a suitable
time for the interview especially in the case of the biggest companies.
In some cases I therefore had to accept a non-actor as the main respondent. I also had to use the telephone in some cases to get the final answers. In the table below the number of respondents - actors and non-
actors - interviewed, face-to-face or by telephone, are summarized:

case no.	actor face-to-face	actor telephone	non-actor face-to-face	non-actor telephone	total number of respondents	total number of actors
1	1		1		2	3
2	1			1	2	3
3	1			1	2	2
4	1				1	1
5	1			1	2	2
6	1			1	2	3
7	1				1	3
8	1				1	4
9	1		1		2	3
10	1				1	3
11	1	1	1		3	2
12		1	2		3	3
13	1		1		2	3
14	3				3	3
15	1			3	4	4
16		1	1	1	3	3
17	1	2			3	3
18	1			1	2	1
19	1			1	2	1
20	1				1	1
21	1		1		2	5
22	1				1	7
23	1				1	1
24	Case eliminated due to lack of actors					
25	1			1	2	1
26	1				1	3
Total	25	5	8	11	49	68

There were thus 26 cases in all. Of these I interviewed 25. The remaining company had been put into liquidation and its managing director and main actor had escaped to southern Europe!

Finally there are a number of possible sources of distortion in this type of retrospective analysis, which need to be commented upon before the results are presented.

First, the possibility of systematic misunderstanding of the answers was reduced by using a number of different assistants that wrote protocols and functioned as discussion partners when the complete questionnaire was being filled in.

The second involved the possibility of making errors in choosing the key actors. The actors were identified in two ways. First, by using the information provided by the different authorities when identifying the cases and, secondly, by tracking them down using the contacts named by the representatives from the Federation of Swedish Industries (Industriförbundet) and the Swedish Export Council (Exportrådet) as starting-points. The character of the questionnaire also made it impossible for a person not involved in the process to answer. On three separate occasions it became apparent that the person being interviewed was not a key actor. In such cases the interview was abandoned.

Thirdly, the fact that not all actors were interviewed must be explained. At an early stage in the study an experiment was conducted. Three main actors in one particular location process were interviewed separately and their answers compared. These were very similar and I concluded from this that the risk of systematic distortion due to interviewing only one actor was small.

"That buzzing-noise means something. You don't get a buzzing-noise like that, just buzzing and buzzing, without its meaning something. If there's a buzzing-noise, somebody's making a buzzing-noise, and the only reason for making a buzzing-noise that I know of is because you're a bee."
(Winnie-the-Pooh)

CHAPTER 5   RESULTS AND ANALYSES

The data acquired will be presented in two ways which complement each other. The first, in chapter 5, aims at analyzing individual variables, factors and also individual relationships. This analysis is based on answers to the questionnaire. The second analysis, in chapter 6, aims basically at grouping the 25 cases in homogeneous "types". This analysis is based on all the data acquired in the course of the field study; not only the answers to the questionnaire. In this chapter appropriate methods to be used when presenting and analyzing the data are discussed and determined. The values and distributions of the six variables, of which two - "location planning" and "performance" - are indicated by more than one attribute, are then described. In the subsequent statistical test only very limited support is obtained. "Physical distance" is significantly correlated with one attribute of "location planning" and three attributes of "location planning" vary significantly with one attribute of the "performance". The remaining components of the extended model, i.e. the 15 proposed relationships, are then analyzed through logical reasoning. A number of interesting conclusions based on the description of the factors are reported but no additional hypotheses are generated. The overall conclusion is that the differences in the cases as mirrored in the data are too large, and the generalities are therefore smoothed out.

115

5.1   Selection of Methods

The methods to be used when analyzing the collected data depend on two things, the kind of data collected and the purpose of the analysis.

First, regarding the character of the data collected, the following comments seem important:

a)   Besides the answers to the questionnaire other data was acquired: through discussions with civil servants when identifying the cases, through discussions with other employees in the companies when identifying the actors, and through informal talks with actors before and after the structured interview.

b)   Some questions are intricate and the quality of the answers strongly depends on the kind of atmosphere and confidence that was created during the discussions. In those few cases when parts of the interview were conducted over the telephone, it was not easy to obtain answers to some critical questions. In a few cases, some questions were not answered at all.

c)   There are many open questions which lead to answers that vary over a wide range of dimensions. The answers thus belong to different types of scale (nominal, ordinal, interval and ratio). The type of scale is closely linked to the concept of measurement. For open questions with verbal answers, measuring cannot readily be performed without categorization (changing from nominal to another kind of scale).

Secondly, regarding the purpose of the analysis, the purpose is to answer the research question from chapter 1: "How can the data from the field study be described and interpreted?" A narrower purpose derived more directly from the empirical research was developed in chapter 4 when determining the appropriate number of cases to investigate:

1.   To describe the variables and the factors; 2. To test the hypotheses; 3. To describe relationships. It was concluded that the last point aimed at the generation of additional hypotheses.

Two different approaches will now be utilized for the analysis of the acquired data.

The approach in chapter 5 can be characterized as a study of the location choice situation in its entirety focusing on individual variables, factors, hypotheses and relations.

In chapter 6 a complementary approach is used for studying the same situation, but here it is done from the viewpoint of the individual cases.

This approach aims at finding similarities in the 25 different location choice situations by grouping them in homogeneous "types". Furthermore the analysis in chapter 6 is based on all the acquired data; not only the answers to the questionnaire. When presenting the results in chapter 6, however, the linkages to the extended model are clearly illustrated. The method of analysis used when developing these "types" will be described in that chapter.

The aim of the present chapter is to analyze components of the extended model. I therefore concentrate here on the three purposes described above. This analysis is based on the collected data expressed in numbers representing the answers to the questionnaire. The design of chapter 5 will be as follows: First the six variables will be described (in 5.2) and then the five hypotheses (H 1 - H 5) tested (in 5.3). Thirdly the suggested factors and relations (R 6 - R 20) will be described (in 5.4).

The methods to be utilized in this chapter will now be determined:

1. To <u>describe the variables,</u> absolute result tables and tables of frequencies will be presented.

In chapter 3 the formulation of the five hypotheses was based on dichotomization: small-large, few-many etc. It should be repeated that the performance variable includes one attribute or question (Q 94) the answer to which is a dichotomy. In the succeeding data presentation, it is therefore also motivated to include original as well as dichotomized variables.

2. To <u>test the hypotheses,</u> somewhat more elaborate methods will be employed. Correlation analysis is useful in specifying the degree of relationships and will therefore be used here. When dealing with the correlation between two relatively continuous distributions, the product-moment (PM) correlation is adequate (Nunnally, 1967, p. 109), if the relation is rectilinear and the scales are interval scales. As the last two of these assumptions can be questioned for some attributes of the studied variables, the rank correlation - which does not require those assumptions - will also be computed.

The independence between variables will also be tested by chi-square calculated from two-by-two tables and using Yate´s correction (Dixon & Massey, 1957, p. 226) as this test does not require that the variables are normally distributed.

There is also another reason to dichotomize. It is easy to conduct a test here called "face test" i.e. a superficial method of analysis. Each case is thus characterized by six 0, 1 variables and evidence in favour of the hypotheses is easy to identify.

The design of the basic model also means that regression analysis can be fruitfully employed here. Such methods often imply causality, while in correlation analysis this is not necessarily the case. Four "independent" variables are in fact assumed to affect the dependent fifth "location planning" variable i.e. H 1, H 2, H 3 and H 4. Furthermore the independent variables in the model are assumed to be independent of each other. This is an assumption in a regression equation as well.

There are a number of other statistical methods that it would be possible to use, but only after a number of severe simplifications and questionable assumptions had been made.

Discriminant analysis, for example, is applicable to problems of this type with the performance variable as the criterion variable. However, more cases are required. The number of variables ought not to exceed the number of cases in the smallest group i.e. "failures" in the performance variable.

One of the underlying motives for using "dimension-reducing methods" as proposed by Green & Carmone (1970, chapter 5), is a desire to summarize the information provided by the whole set of cases. The use of variables/factors produces a more concise structure which removes redundancy in the original set of data and/or attempts to preserve most of the information contained in the original data matrix. This method, which is not utilized here, is thus a means of data-reduction and summary. The intention of the method is to reduce manifest data, portrayed as cases in variable space, into a space of fewer dimensions, with minimum loss of information.

The complementary method is to reduce the number of cases by dividing them into homogeneous groups, based on their "closeness" to one another in variable space. The first approach may be called "reduced space analysis" and the second "cluster analysis" (ibid., p. 97). The reason why these two approaches are not used here is basically the existence of great numbers of open questions with consequent scaling problems. It must also be remembered that this study only includes 25 cases which are therefore easy to grasp.

In conclusion, the methods used in section 5.3 will be: correlation analysis, "face test", chi-square analysis and regression analysis.

118

3.   The purpose of <u>description of factors and relationships</u> will be explained by reasoned argument. Since the approach is fact-finding,
which in this case means description of the factors rather than an ende-
avour to obtain measurements, statistical methods are not relevant. In
fact the purpose is not to test hypotheses but to refine the questions and
possibly to generate hypotheses. Although in some limited number of
relationships it would, in principle, be possible to conduct correlation
analysis, this will be left for future research.

5.2   Description of Variables

In this section values, distributions and also some limitations will be
presented. The ways of setting the limits will be called "artificial"
and "natural" dichotomization respectively. In the artificial method all
scores below the median are coded zero, and all scores at or above the
median are coded 1 (this method is based on roughly equally sized
classes). The natural dichotomization, occurring in the fourth and
sixth of the variables presented below, is based on a logical division.

Starting with the first variable: The location choice situation has been
defined as making a site selection in interaction with seven other
selections, such as selection of product and selection of capacity. If in
the last category the number of selections not finally made is high when
the search for a site starts, this is likely to complicate the search.
The degree of this phenomenon is indicated through the <u>complexity</u>
variable.

Complexity	0	1	2	3	4	5	6	7
Number of cases	3	11	2	4	2	2	1	0
Dichotomy	Few (F)		Many (M)					

If the number of decision variables is 0 or 1, the case will be classified
as "few" = F as shown in the table above. If the number is 2 or more,
the complexity will be indicated in this artificial dichotomization as
"many" = M. This gives 14 F and 11 M.

The second variable concerns the management style which is indicated
by the <u>number</u> of participants or <u>actors</u> employed by the firm on the
selection process (Q 5). Since there is a large group in "the middle",
12 cases with 3 actors, this variable is difficult to dichotomize. The
distribution is:

119

Number of actors	1	2	3	4	5	6	7
Number of cases	6	3	12	2	1	0	1
Dichotomy	Few (F)			Many (M)			

The table also shows the dichotomy Few-Many.

The third variable expresses the extent to which the company has negotiated with authorities about subsidies and other advantages (Q 34, Q 35).

This <u>negotiation contacts</u> variable includes

a)   all sites considered preceding and including the selected one

b)   contacts on different levels: e.g. with local authorities concerning prices of and facilities attached to sites and buildings, housing quotas and rents for plants, with the National Labour Market Board (Arbetsmarknadsstyrelsen, AMS) and the Trade Development Associations concerning loans, and with the Ministry of Finance concerning the use of investment funds

c)   all kinds of contacts, face-to-face as well as by telephone and letter.

In some cases the respondent expressed the answer in other measures than hours. I will therefore make the assumption that "one day" is equivalent to 8 hours and "one week" to 40 hours of negotiation contacts. In the table below the cases are distributed in intervals. The number of contacts is thus translated into hours of contacts.

Hours of contacts	0-9	10-19	20-29	30-39	40-49	50-59	60-69	70-79	80-89	90-99	100-199	200-299	300-399	≥ 400
Number of cases	5	4	3	2	3	1	0	0	2	1	1	0	2	1
Dichotomy	Few (F)		Many (M)											

The fourth variable is the <u>physical distance</u> and indicates the extent to which the selected site is known a priori. The road distance between the actors´ office and the selected site is measured in kilometres (Q 42).

Number of kilometres	0-90	100-199	200-299	300-399	400-499	500-599	600-699	700-799	800-899	≥ 900
Number of cases	3	4	7	2	2	2	2	1	0	2
Dichotomy	Small (S)		Large (L)							

In this case the dichotomy is natural (not artificial). The limit is determined by the estimated commuting distance (returning the same day).

The fifth variable is the <u>location planning</u> which is defined in four ways. A. The "source" definition; B. The "model of systematic behaviour" definition; C. The "cost" definition; D. The "time" definition.

A.   All the 27 "pieces of data" in the questionnaire were identified in the six cases in chapter 2.   It is assumed that these are value free. This measure tells us if any of the actors came in contact with or used any of these 27 items during the location planning.   A large number of affirmatives i.e. a large data base is equivalent to large-scale location planning and vice versa (Q 57).

Number of "pieces of data"	≤ 5	6	7	8	9	10	11	12	13	14	15	16	17	18	19	20	≥ 21
Number of cases	0	3	2	4	2	0	0	0	3	3	0	0	2	3	2	1	0
Dichotomy	Small (S)							Large (L)									

B.   The second instrument for measuring the location planning is the congruence of each case with the "model of systematic behaviour".   A large number of affirmatives in this case indicates that the individual decision behaviour is systematic (Q 62) i.e. large-scale location planning.

Number of "yes"	0	1	2	3	4	5	6
Number of cases	0	8	6	1	3	5	2
Dichotomy	Small (S)			Large (L)			

C. The third definition of location planning is the total amount of money spent on preparing the location decision. Here all activities, negotiations as well as data collection, are included. Since the answers varied as far as the descriptions were concerned, the following assumptions and standards will be introduced. The cost of location planning, i.e. the salary for one day, is 400 Skr and for one week 2,000 Skr. Since most of the visits were made by car, I have estimated the travel expenses at 5 Skr per 10 kilometres. With these assumptions, the following distribution summarizes the results. The costs are expressed in thousands of kronor (Q 63).

Total cost	1	2	3	4	5	6	7	8	9	10	11	12	13	14	15-19	20-49	50-99	100-199	≥200
Number of cases	1	0	2	0	3	2	1	2	0	4	0	1	0	0	2	2	2	1	2
Dichotomy	Small (S)				Large (L)														

D. The last attribute indicating the location planning is the time devoted to it. The total time expressed in months starts when the question of location was mentioned for the first time (t_1) and ends at the time of the formal decision (t_2). In some cases, when the respondents only remembered the year of t_1, I have counted the number of months from July of that year (Q 66 – Q 68).

Number of months	1	2	3	4	5	6	7	8	9	10	11	12	13	14	15-19	20-49	50-99	≥100
Number of cases	1	3	2	0	1	1	1	2	0	1	0	2	1	1	2	3	3	1
Dichotomy	Small (S)				Large (L)													

122

In order to investigate the similarity of the four definitions the abbreviations: L = Large and S = Small will be used.

The 25 cases identified in chapter 4 will now be given new sequential numbers and will also be arranged in a random way to avoid all possibility of identification.

The variable: Location planning

Case number	A. The "source" definition	B. The "model of systematic behavior" definition	C. The "cost" definition	D. The "time" definition
1	13/27 L	2/6 S	18 L	10 L
2	6/27 S	1/6 S	12 L	2 S
3	8/27 S	2/6 S	6 S	64 L
4	6/27 S	1/6 S	10 L	13 L
5	13/27 L	6/6 L	50 L	12 L
6	8/27 S	1/6 S	5 S	19 L
7	9/27 S	1/6 S	1 S	2 S
8	14/27 L	4/6 L	6 S	3 S
9	9/27 S	2/6 S	3 S	5 S
10	8/27 S	1/6 S	10 L	112 L
11	14/27 L	5/6 L	5 S	31 L
12	7/27 S	2/6 S	3 S	15 L
13	19/27 L	5/6 L	100 L	60 L
14	6/27 S	1/6 S	8 S	2 S
15	17/27 L	4/6 L	5 S	28 L
16	18/27 L	6/6 L	15 L	7 S
17	18/27 L	5/6 L	75 L	65 L
18	8/27 S	2/6 S	8 S	8 S
19	14/27 L	5/6 L	200 L	14 L
20	20/27 L	5/6 L	210 L	37 L
21	13/27 L	1/6 S	7 S	1 S
22	17/27 L	4/6 L	35 L	6 S
23	18/27 L	1/6 S	25 L	8 S
24	19/27 L	3/6 L	10 L	12 L
25	7/27 S	2/6 S	10 L	3 S

The consonance between the dichotomized operational variables in all
possible combinations is rather high, especially between A and B.
Since the number of cases in the two classes differs, the theoretical
consonance also differs. This is considered in the brief consonance
test that is shown below.

AB = 22/22 means 22 fits out of 22 etc, BC = 16/22, CD = 15/25,
AC = 17/25, BD = 16/22, AD = 15/25, ABC = 15/22, BCD = 11/22,
ACD = 11/25, ABCD = 10/22.

The sixth variable – performance – is measured by means of six attributes. In this case the dichotomy is arrived at by dividing the population into "successful" and "unsuccessful" locations.

A.   The first attribute is based on the question: Was the plant, after the
running-in period and purely from a geographical point of view, with a
summarized judgement, either very successful (= 1), very unsuccessful (= 5) or somewhere between (= 2-4). The dichotomy will be (Q 89):

Success: 1, 2, 3

Failure: 4, 5

B.   The second attribute is based on the question: What was the average
unit cost (x) for the principal product in the new plant after the running-
in period (t_4)? This cost is expressed as a percentage of the actual
average cost at t_2 (Q 83):

Success: if the average unit cost (x) $\leq$ 100

Failure: if the average unit cost (x) $>$ 100

C.   The answers to the five questions measuring the degrees to which
expectations were met with respect to production volume, turnover,
new employees, profitability (productivity) and product line are given
weights. The average of these weights is then used for dichotomization.
The dichotomy will be the following: supposing 1 is equivalent to much
larger, 5 to much less and 2-4 somewhere between (Q 84, Q 85, Q 86,
Q 87, Q 88):

Success: $\leq$ 3
Failure: $>$ 3

D.   A further expression of the extent to which expectations were met deals with the difference between the actual average unit cost at t_4 (x) and the projected average unit cost at t_4 estimated at t_2 (y). The following limits are assumed (Q 82, Q 83):

Success: if x-y or y-x ≤ 15

Failure: if x-y or y-x > 15

E.   The scoring model (Q 90, Q 91, Q 92, Q 93) is based on four fac-tors identified and ranked by the actors. Each factor is then estimated along a five-point scale. The factor weight is multiplied by the scale item and these four numbers are finally added. The range of the total sum is then 10-50 and the dichotomy used is:

Success: if the number of points is 39-50

Failure: if the number of points is 10-38

F.   The final attribute is indicated through an indirect question: "If you were to make the same location decision today, would you select the same place? (Q 94) Yes or no. The dichotomy is:

Success: Yes

Failure: No

Finally the performance profile of each case will be presented.

The consonance between the alternative attributes constituting the cri-teria of performance seems even greater than the consonance between the definitions of location planning. The total number of possible com-binations of attributes is too large, and therefore only the pairs will be examined. But before this it should be pointed out that there are three full rows of failures (12, 16 and 23) and six with only indications of success (cases 1, 3, 8, 10, 15 and 25). Considering the different number of observations in the dichotomies the pair-wise results show:

AB = 19/19, AC = 17/17, AD = 20/20, AE = 19/19, AF = 21/21,
BC = 17/27, BD = 20/24, BE = 19/25, BF = 17/23, CD = 18/22,
CE = 15/23, CF = 17/21, DE = 18/24, DF = 18/24, EF = 19/23

In the table below the results of all cases and all attributes are presen-ted in absolute as well as dichotomized values:

125

The variable: Performance

Case number	A. "geographical"		y/x	B. x	C. "expectations are met"		D. x-y or y-x		E. "scoring model"		F. "simulating the earlier situation"	
1	2	S	100/100	S	3	S	0	S	50	S	yes	S
2	2	S	85/95	S	3.5	F	10	S	43	S	yes	S
3	2	S	95/90	S	2	S	5	S	47	S	yes	S
4	2	S	70/90	S	1	S	20	F	42	S	yes	S
5	1	S	100/120	F	4	F	20	F	39	S	yes	S
6	2	S	120/180	F	1.5	S	60	F	36	F	yes	S
7	2	S	70/80	S	3	S	10	S	33	F	yes	S
8	3	S	90/90	S	3	S	0	S	42	S	yes	S
9	1	S	90/90	S	1	S	0	S	43	S	no	F
10	1	S	100/85	S	2	S	15	S	49	S	yes	S
11	3	S	85/105	F	4	F	20	F	31	F	no	F
12	5	F	100/190	F	3.5	F	90	F	16	F	no	F
13	3	S	95/98	S	3.5	F	3	S	25	F	no	F
14	2	S	95/105	F	2	S	10	S	42	S	yes	S
15	1	S	98/95	S	2	S	3	S	45	S	yes	S
16	4	F	95/125	F	4	F	30	F	17	F	no	F
17	3	S	80/100	S	5	F	20	F	44	S	yes	S
18	3	S	100/100	S	3.5	F	0	S	46	S	yes	S
19	1	S	80/70	S	3	S	10	S	36	F	yes	S
20	3	S	110/110	F	2.5	S	0	S	29	F	yes	S
21	2	S	90/90	S	2	S	0	S	39	S	no	F
22	1	S	85/95	S	4	F	10	S	41	S	yes	S
23	4	F	100/130	F	5	F	30	F	21	F	**no**	F
24	2	S	100/110	F	4	F	10	S	44	S	yes	S
25	1	S	90/75	S	1	S	15	S	39	S	yes	S

5.3   Test of the Hypotheses

In this section the six variables presented will be brought together and a base for a test of the proposed relationships will be constructed. However the hypotheses will first be repeated.

H 1 (hypothesis 1): The degree of "complexity" is negatively related to the amount of "location planning".

H 2:   The "number of actors" is positively related to the amount of "location planning".

H 3:   The number of hours for "negotiation contacts" is negatively related to the amount of "location planning".

H 4:   The size of the "physical distance" is positively related to the amount of "location planning".

H 5:   The amount of "location planning" is positively related to the "performance" i.e. the greater the amount of location planning the higher the probability of success, and the smaller the amount of location planning the higher the probability of failure.

These five hypotheses will be tested in different ways. As stated earlier the following methods will be used:

1.   Correlation analysis

2.   "Face test" and chi-square analysis

3.   Regression analysis

1.   Correlation analysis

The hypotheses H 1, H 2, H 3 and H 4 will first be tested using four attributes of the variable "location planning" separately. (The computer program: BMD 02 R - Stepwise regression - revised July 17, 1970. Health sciences computing facility, UCLA is used). In the correlation matrix below the results containing product-moment (PM) correlations are presented:

		Complexity	Number of actors	Negotiation contacts	Physical distance
Location planning	A. The "source" definition	−0.351	0.040	0.376	0.399+
	B. The "model of systematic beha- viour" definition	−0.323	−0.014	0.279	0.062
	C. The "cost" definition	−0.166	−0.308	0.670+++	0.220
	D. The "time" definition	−0.093	−0.091	0.085	−0.151

+ and +++ indicate correlations that are significant at the 5 % and
0.1 % level respectively.

The degree of "complexity" is negatively correlated with all four attributes of "location planning". This is in agreement with H 1. However
none of the correlations are statistically significant.

The correlations between the "number of actors" and "location planning"
are insignificant and do not support H 2 especially as the numerically
largest correlation coefficient is negative.

The number of hours spent in "negotiation contacts" is positively
correlated with all four attributes of "location planning", the correlation with cost being highly significant. Thus H 3 should be rejected
and replaced by the reversed hypothesis i.e. that the amount of negotiation is positively correlated with the amount of "location planning".

The correlation between "physical distance" and data base is positive
and significant at the 5 % level, but the correlations between "physical
distance" and the three other attributes of "location planning" are weak
and insignificant. Thus H 4 has only limited support.

Next, the correlation between "location planning" and "performance"
i.e. H 5, will be investigated. Since four of the six attributes (A, C,
E and F) of the performance variable are ordinal scales rank correlations will be computed. The (4 x 4 =) 16 rank correlation scores are
presented in the table below together with all possible product-moment
correlations.

128

Performance

Location planning	A. "geographical" [1]		B. x	C. "expectations are met"		D. x-y or y-x	E. "scoring model"		F. "simulating the earlier situation"	
	Rank	(PM)	PM	Rank	(PM)	PM	Rank	(PM)	Rank	(PM)
A. The "source" definition	0.210	(0.263)	-0.025	0.550++	(0.577++)	0.098	-0.259	(-0.297)	-0.230	(-0.214)
B. The "model of systematic behaviour" definition	0.100	(0.120)	-0.049	0.476+	(0.464+)	0.062	-0.221	(-0.271)	-0.095	(-0.092)
C. The "cost" definition	-0.014	(0.019)	-0.159	0.409+	(0.155)	0.213	-0.094	(-0.211)	0.161	(0.122)
D. The "time" definition	-0.043	(0.113)	-0.096	0.094	(0.005)	0.191	-0.082	(0.163)	0.056	(0.080)

+ and ++ indicate correlations that are significant at the 5 % and 1 % level respectively

1/ For this performance attribute a high score indicates failure whereas for the remaining performance attributes a high score indicates success.

The heterogeneity is obvious and the hypothesis H 5 is not supported. Irrespective of which operational measures are combined, no regularities seem to appear. However the two types of correlation, Rank and PM, show great similarities. One is led to conclude that good planning – by my definition – is no guarantee of success.

2. "Face test" and chi-square analysis

These methods are based on the earlier presented dichotomization. In order to simplify the analysis, the variables of "location planning" and "performance" will be indicated by the "source" definition which was the original operational variable from chapter 2, and by the attribute A. "geographical" which will be considered to be the best representation of the performance variable.

First the superficial "face test" (which should not be confused with the established sign-test) is described. The total set of numbers, including the 0, 1 variable signs, are summarized in the table below. Each of the 25 cases is examined regarding the five hypotheses. A plus indicates a correct hypothesis and a minus an incorrect hypothesis.

Case number	Variables											Hypotheses				
	Complexity		Number of actors		Negotiation contacts		Physical distance		Location planning A. The "source" definition		Performance A. "geo-graphical"		H1	H2	H3	H4	H5
1	0	F	3	M	80	M	13	S	13	L	2	S	+	+	–	–	+
2	4	M	3	M	16	F	26	L	6	S	2	S	+	–	–	–	–
3	3	M	2	F	48	M	38	L	8	S	2	S	+	+	+	–	–
4	1	F	1	F	14	F	9	S	6	S	2	S	–	+	–	+	–
5	0	F	2	F	376	M	47	L	13	L	1	S	+	–	–	+	+
6	1	F	3	M	0	F	14	S	8	S	2	S	–	–	–	+	–
7	2	M	3	M	35	M	5	S	9	S	2	S	+	–	+	+	–
8	1	F	4	M	13	F	41	L	14	L	3	S	+	+	+	+	+
9	2	M	3	M	3	F	11	S	9	S	1	S	+	–	–	+	–
10	2	M	3	M	0	F	14	S	8	S	1	S	+	–	–	+	–
11	1	F	2	F	45	M	24	L	14	L	3	S	+	–	–	+	+
12	5	M	3	M	0	F	70	L	7	S	5	F	+	–	–	–	+
13	1	F	3	M	40	M	22	L	19	L	3	S	+	+	–	+	+
14	3	M	3	M	152	M	37	L	6	S	2	S	+	–	+	–	–
15	6	M	4	M	33	M	28	L	17	L	1	S	–	+	–	+	+
16	1	F	3	M	17	F	21	L	18	L	4	F	+	+	+	+	–
17	0	F	3	M	80	M	25	L	18	L	3	S	+	+	–	+	+
18	4	M	1	F	27	F	69	L	8	S	3	S	+	+	–	–	–
19	3	M	1	F	96	M	58	L	14	L	1	S	–	–	–	+	+
20	1	F	1	F	2,080	M	66	L	20	L	3	S	+	–	–	+	+
21	5	M	5	M	28	F	29	L	13	L	2	S	–	+	+	+	+
22	1	F	7	M	55	M	53	L	17	L	1	S	+	+	–	+	+
23	1	F	1	F	360	M	138	L	18	L	4	F	+	–	–	+	–
24	0	F	1	F	29	F	94	L	19	L	2	S	+	–	+	+	+
25	1	F	3	M	3	F	0	S	7	S	1	S	–	–	–	+	–
													19+	11+	7+	19+	13+

This superficial "face test" on the data collected does not indicate complete verification of any of the suggested relationships. The hypotheses H 1 and H 4, however, are supported by 19 out of 25 cases (and 19 out of 21, if the different sizes of the classes are taken into consideration). With respect to H 2, the number of actors does not, in this empirical setting, seem to be related to the amount of "location planning" (11 out of 23). The number of hours spent in "negotiation contacts" tends to vary positively with the amount of "location planning" (7 cases out of 23), which agrees with the finding of the correlation analysis. The conclusion is therefore that "economic business strategy" and "political strategy" are not exclusive but occur simultaneously. Thus hypothesis H 3, as well as H 2, is once again proved wrong. As to the relationship between the two variables "location planning" and "performance", this empirical investigation does not give any clear pattern.

The chi-square method is applicable to only one of the five hypotheses, H 3, since the "minimum theoretical frequency for the 2 x 2 table should not be less than 5" (Dixon & Massey, 1957, p. 226). If the required probability for significance is "only" less than 0.10, the correlation is significant. However, H 3 is rejected as the correlation is positive and not negative as stated in the hypothesis.

3. Regression analysis

"Location planning" is in this case assumed to be a dependent variable while "complexity", "number of actors", "negotiation contacts" and "physical distance" are independent. These assumptions were introduced when the basic model was built in chapter 2. Now, however, the relationships are assumed in addition to be additive. If the five variables mentioned are called LP, CO, AC, NC and PD, the model may be represented by the following symbols:

$$LP = a + b_1 CO + b_2 AC + b_3 NC + b_4 PD$$

"a" is the value that the equation predicts for LP when CO, AC, NC and PD are all zero; a situation which never occurs in reality. Thus the value of "a" is of no concern.

The regression equation is constructed by using the above mentioned stepwise computer program. The four steps will appear thus:

1. $LP = 10.0 + 0.06\ PD$ $R = 0.40$

2. $LP = 12.0 + 0.06\ PD - 1.02\ CO$ $R = 0.54$

3. $LP = 8.84 + 0.08\ PD - 1.18\ CO + 1.03\ AC$ $R = 0.60$

4. $LP = 7.97 + 0.07\ PD - 1.06\ CO + 1.23\ AC + 0.003\ NC$ $R = 0.66$

The signs of the regression coefficients are in accordance with all the hypotheses except H 3.

In the first two steps the coefficient for PD is significant at the 5 % level. In the second step the coefficient for CO is not significant at the 5 % level but at the 10 % level.

In the third step the coefficients for PD and CO are both significant at the 5 % level. The coefficient for AC, however is, not significant $(0.20 < p < 0.30)$.

Also in the fourth step the coefficients for PD and CO are significant at the 5 % level. Here AC is significant at the 10 % level, but NC is not significant $(0.10 < p < 0.20)$.

Finally, the equation should not be used for extrapolation beyond the range of the observed values.

5.4 Descriptions of the Relationships

Having investigated those variables and that category of relationships which are called hypotheses, the factors and remaining relationships (R 6 - R 20) included in the extended model will be described in this section. The potential amount of factor and variable combinations is extremely large, even if only pairs are considered. For this reason, only a limited number of relationships will be examined. A secondary aim here is to acquire evidence for the formulation of additional hypotheses.

The method of presentation will be based not on statistical methods, but on logical reasoning. In addition the material will be divided into two parts. The first one, which is presented in this section, is predominately verbal and includes some summarizing graphs illustrating the frequency distributions of answers. The second one consists of a data list. The raw data are presented in the data list made up of 15 tables, which is available on request.

The design of the sub-section describing the 15 relationships, R 6 - R 20, will be as follows: First, the answers to the relevant questions are described. Secondly, the proposed relationship is commented upon using the answers as a background.

Not unexpectedly, there are a large number of reasons why most of the locations were initiated and carried through. Though it is difficult to get a true picture of the network of causes and effects that have gone to make up these reasons, the "lack-of-labour" argument was the one mentioned most frequently, though in different contexts, during the interviews.

In an attempt to structure the answers, I have tried to identify the most important reasons: These reasons are then grouped into 13 categories. Then the categories are dichotomized into "pull" factors (10 categories and 17 cases) and "push" factors (5 categories and 8 cases). In this somewhat arbitrary dichotomization, the push factors represent a change in the environment system, while the pull factors emanate from within the company or location management systems.

Pull	Number of cases
Lack of labour in combination with expansion plans	4
New product that needs to be further developed	3
Signed joint venture in combination with fast expansion	2
Dissatisfaction with the old job creates new establishment plans	2
Expansion in another place in order to ease the pressure of demand on labour	1
More capacity	1
Large order	1
New markets estimated as good	1
New product for which the transportation possibilities are inconvenient	1
A depot in Sweden	1
	17

134

Push	Number of cases
Inner milieu i.e. old, worn out and noisy localities	3
Financing of other projects	2
The labour supply diminishes	1
The labour union suspects "grey labour"	1
New place where a new production technology can be built up	1
	8

The historical conditions are a very interesting factor, which can probably explain a lot more about the form and content of location planning than was previously thought.

The second aspect of this factor concerns the alternatives to a new location which were discussed. Rather few such alternatives (only 13 of the 25 cases) were in fact mentioned. These alternatives can be distributed according to another classification as shown below.

Expansion in the existing place	5
Do nothing - stay on the old job (for actors thinking of starting new establishments)	3
Buy the products from somewhere else	2
Expansion in other plants within the company	1
Close down the product line	1
Acquire temporary housing	1
	13

Thirdly, it was asked what steps were taken to avoid a location. In 21 cases no actions were taken at all. One firm stressed its attempts to utilize the existing production capacity for as long as possible. In one case the labour force tried to prevent a branch from being located. They argued that quality would be lowered, but they were also worried about their future employment situation. In the two remaining cases, the labour union strongly opposed the location decision, criticizing it openly. And in one of these the union obviously stopped a total relocation of the plant, since only a minor part of it was located.

The differences between the cases are pronounced, and it is impossible to draw any general conclusions. The proposed relation R 6 has therefore not received any clear support from this data and no additional hypothesis is formulated.

R 7: Actor´s attitude towards secrecy - number of actors

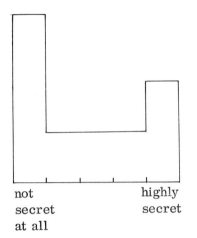

not
secret
at all

highly
secret

In 10 of the 25 cases the location problem was regarded as highly secret and in 6 cases as not secret at all. The secrecy argument thus seems relevant. Looking at the correlation, however, there is no clear pattern.

R 8: Company characteristics - number of actors

Here six subfactors are identified. The number of employees, the turnover, the ownership, the goals, the number of located firms (organizational experience) and the degree of centralization.

Of these subfactors, none shows a pattern that gives evidence for a hypothesis.

The population is dominated by big firms. There are 15 cases with more than 400 employees and ten with less. Of these 15 companies, ten are quoted on the Stock Market. With respect to goals, in eight cases "growth" is ranked as the main target. However, no very clear picture emerges, since in eight cases the respondents preferred not to rank at all, or mentioned other goals than those proposed by me, or would not answer at all.

The subfactor "number of new plants" differs widely. In 13 cases, no plant had been established during the last decade. Five firms had located one plant, and each of the remaining seven firms two plants or more.

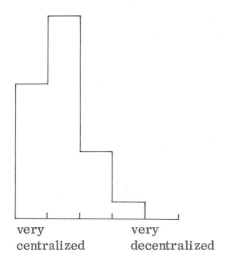

The question on the extent to which the company is centralized revealed a general tendency to centralization. The distribution of answers is shown in the diagram.

very   very
centralized   decentralized

R 9: Size of location project - number of actors

Neither the number of employees nor the turnover in the located plant show any correlation with the number of actors. Surprisingly enough this size variable yields as little explanation as the "company characteristics". The number of actors thus does not vary with the absolute size of the company or with the size indices of the actual location project. The figures of growth of these indices also show great heterogeneity.

R 10: Number of actors - conflicts between actors

According to the answers given no severe conflicts seem to have occurred. However, here the shortcomings of the data-collection method must be taken into account. Other more clinically oriented methods are required to get the true answers to these questions.

It is worth noting that the disparities mentioned did not in any of the cases concern the choice between different sites. Some other sources of conflict were mentioned, such as to invest or not to invest, the layout of the plant, production, sales etc.

In 15 cases no disparity of views was mentioned at all.

Any correlation between the proposed factor and the variable "number of actors" is not supported by this data.

Actors´ behaviour is broken down into three categories or subfactors.
First, the identity of the person who mentioned the concept of location
for the first time was sought. The result shows that in 17 cases an
actor was the initiator, which is not surprising. The reason is that a
location project is often a complicated and risky project which requires
power but also, basically, motivation. Of the remaining cases, six
were initiated by non-actors and two "just evolved".

The second subfactor concerns the identification of forces – impetus or
change forces and status quo forces – underlying the location process.
The results are very disappointing, since in most cases the respondents did not answer (which could indicate irrelevance of the question).
The most reasonable interpretation however, is that such factors are
very important but somewhat difficult to catch during a snapshot case-
study of this type.

Thirdly, the pattern of visiting behaviour or search pattern is briefly
characterized from the answers to a few questions. In nine of the cases
only one place was visited; the one that was selected. There are two
extremes where 15 and 17 different places were considered, while in
nine cases between two and six places were visited. In two cases the
selected places were known by the actors because there were already
plants there owned by the mother company. A definite conclusion is
that actors have selected the last place visited in time. This was the
case in all but two cases. Nearly all visits were one-day visits made
by the actors. The evaluation of sites seems to have been done simultaneously. Immediately after the visit the alternative was eliminated.
In a few cases they were retained and were assessed in competition with
alternatives generated later. The total number of man-days spent on
different sites during the location planning varies but is strikingly small.

The correlation naturally does not exist since we lack data on the conflict variable.

R 12: Actors´ background characteristics – actors´ behaviour

The background of each actor is operationalized along three lines:
occupation, education and experience. Starting with occupation the
total class of 68 actors (all men) is dominated by two groups: production
managers and managing directors. The table below shows the distribution. In fact the titles given in the interviews vary a lot but are classified into 12 categories.

Occupation	Number of actors
Production manager	23
Managing director	19
Financial manager	6
Staff planner	5
Vice managing director	3
Constructor	3
Investment manager	3
Chairman of the board	2
Personnel manager	1
Purchase manager	1
Works manager	1
Outside consultant	1
	68

There are three types of actor combinations involved in the "location management system".

Type 1: production manager/financial manager/managing director

Type 2: managing director

Type 3: a number of production managers

The role of the financial managers is - surprisingly - to formulate contracts and to handle general legal matters. This could be interpreted as showing that location planning is not primarily an economic problem. The table further reveals that there were 61 managers involved and only seven planners.

The second classification - education - gave the following results:

139

Formal education	Number of actors
Graduate engineer	32
Technician	11
Engineer	9
"Civilekonom"	6
Only obligatory school	5
"Ekonom"	3
"Jur kand"	1
"Fil mag"	1
	68

The group is clearly very much dominated by technically educated people, which is interesting. There are a number of possible explanations for this. Since the top managers of this generation were generally educated at technical high schools, it is reasonable to assume that a high proportion of the actors were originally technicians (it is only in recent years that the number of graduates from business schools has become significant). Another explanation is that since the proportion of technicians employed in the mechanical engineering industry is high, the proportion in the location management systems of the same industry will be high as well. A third explanation is that the location problem is regarded as a technical problem and that is why it is given to technically skilled people.

Thirdly, the actors´ experience of location problems and of other unstructured problems was investigated. The answers are not easy to interpret. Usually the respondent described the total number of years he had worked in business. The kind of location problem and the kind of job they had been involved in differed very much. One conclusion here, however, is that it is very difficult to separate the search for a site from other kinds of jobs closely linked to the real location problem. Of the 68 actors, 39 had some kind of experience of location problem. Out of the remaining 29, 16 had no experience. In 13 cases no answer was given since the respondent did not have that information about his colleagues. This lack of knowledge was even more extreme when questions were asked about other types of experience and in some cases the answers were too unclear for any comparison to be possible.

R 13: Sources of finance - amount of money received/condition

The basic question here is: Do firms with other sources of finance have to care that much about subsidies? This difficult question is answered

in an indirect way by examining the actual method of financing the new
site and building as well as the sums received after negotiations.

These subsidies are thus limited to those incentive schemes relevant
for site and building. It must be pointed out that, in addition to these
pecuniary advantages, the respondents frequently talked about housing
for the labour force promised by the local authorities. This advantage
was seldom formally confirmed. Another kind of advantage was favourable renting deals with the local authority. Though this subject was
often discussed, it is difficult to quantify. Many of the firms also received educational grants, but no firm mentioned this as an argument
when choosing between sites. In all cases but four, this grant was formally decided upon after the site was finally chosen. The transportation
grant, a further kind of subsidy, was not mentioned by any firm as relevant when searching for a site.

Finally, state locational grants and loans applicable to machines and
tools have not been included in the description below.

The financing of the new site and building is summarized:

The source of finance	Number of cases
Rented	12
100 % internal means	3
Internal means + investment fund	3
100 % investment fund	3
Internal means + location grant/loan	2
100 % location grant/loan	1
100 % bank loan	1
	25

This table can be further reduced, according to the occurrence of the
two state schemes – investment funds, and location grant and/or loan:

Investment funds	7
Location grant/loan	3
Nothing	15
	25

In most cases (12) there is no financing when the firm rents. A second
step in the life of a branch however, is when a new factory is built.
This step had been taken in some of the cases. It is interesting to note
that in 15 of the cases no Government subsidies are involved at all.

Looking more closely at the subsidies, one finds that the total amount of investment fund released is 65.5 million Skr. The total sum of location loans is 16.5 million Skr and the location grants 2.4 million Skr. The investment funds are subject to conditions formulated by the Ministry of Finance. These are based on the law which states that investment funds can be used in regional policy. In four of the investment fund cases the firms have consequently been obliged to employ a specific number of people. Furthermore, in some cases, the company must accept a specific place for the establishment in order to get the fund released.

R 14: Amount of money received/condition - negotiation contacts

The collected data gives no support for causality. On the contrary, the cases where investment funds are used tend to be related to small numbers of "negotiation contacts". This raises the issue of the type of contact and the negotiators rather than the duration of the contact.

R 15: Actors who negotiate - amount of money received/condition

The managing director was involved in six of the 10 cases where investment funds or location loans/grants were received. In the cases involving investment funds, the project is first looked upon as an investment or finance problem and is only seen as a location problem after preliminary contacts between the principal actors and the Ministry of Finance have revealed that locating to a specific site constitutes a condition for using the investment funds.

It must be pointed out that there are negotiations on different levels in the firm and that the description here only concerns the object of the site and building.

The Ministry of Finance normally has direct discussions with the managing director of large firms. These discussions are short, one or two hours only. There are often one to three such discussions that concern the total investment program where the branch location only constitutes a minor part.

There is no sign of any further pattern to support hypotheses about this proposed relationship.

R 16: Conflicts between authorities - negotiation contacts

A common answer to questions about conflict, was: "No, not that we know". My conviction is that it is difficult to identify any sort of conflict in a discussion as short as these interviews.

142

In five cases conflicts were mentioned. Only in three cases, however, did these concern the question of site selection. There is thus no base for creating a hypothesis.

R 17: Classification of area in which site is located - physical distance

I would suggest that the a priori intention to move to a Development Area is correlated with the physical distance involved. This relationship is not easy to confirm even if it seems reasonable.

R 18: Attitudes to different areas - physical distance

The purpose of this section is to describe, using 13 questions, the attitudes of the group of principal actors represented by the respondents. In the presentation below the question is followed by a histogram illustrating the frequency of answers. The differences refer to the new location.

The difference between various places in Sweden are generally (Q 44)

The difference between a place within the Development Area and a place outside is generally (Q 45)

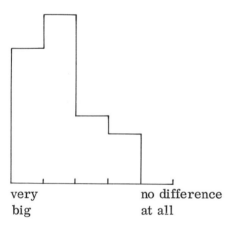

very   no difference
big   at all

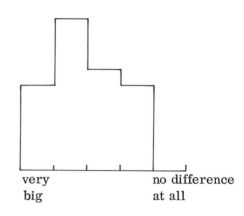

very   no difference
big   at all

The difference between a place within a "big town area" (Stockholm, Gothenburg and Malmö) and a place elsewhere is generally (Q 46)

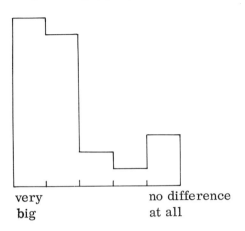

very big — no difference at all

The difference between a place in Norrland and a place elsewhere in the country is generally (Q 47)

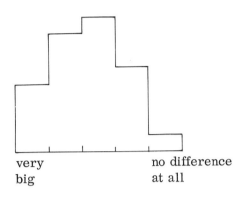

very big — no difference at all

The difference between a place in Svealand and a place elsewhere is generally (Q 48)

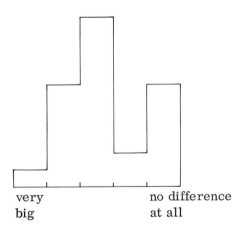

very big — no difference at all

The difference between a place in Götaland and a place elsewhere is generally (Q 49)

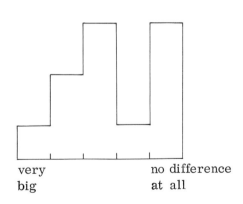

very big — no difference at all

The differences between sites within various counties are generally (Q 50)

The differences between sites within various municipalities are generally (Q 51)

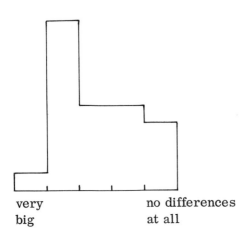

very
big

no differences
at all

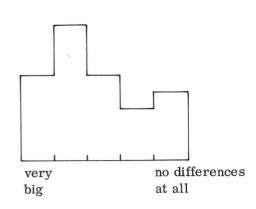

very
big

no differences
at all

The remaining five questions:

Small places are avoided because the social responsibility can be too big and the future flexibility of the plant therefore reduced (Q 52)

Some places are avoided because the prevailing industrial tradition is limited (Q 53)

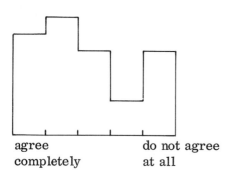

agree
completely

do not agree
at all

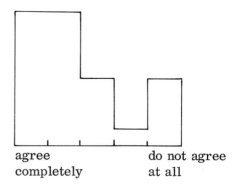

agree
completely

do not agree
at all

Big places are preferred because the potential labour supply is bigger despite the fact the labour mobility often is higher (Q 54)

You would decide to locate a plant in an isolated place in order to be alone in the place and therefore not have to compete for labour (Q 55)

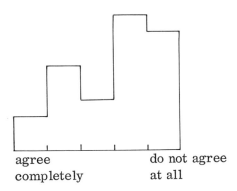

agree
completely

do not agree
at all

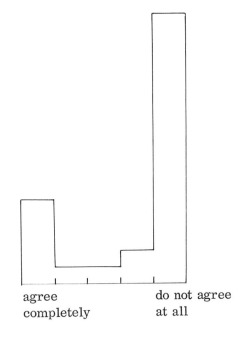

agree
completely

do not agree
at all

Certain places are avoided because the prevailing attitude there towards industry in general is negative (Q 56)

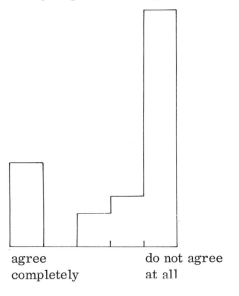

agree
completely

do not agree
at all

The pressure of competition experienced on the "product market", the "labour market" and on "other resource markets" vary strikingly. Another conclusion is that the average competition for labour is higher than other types of competition.

No clear pattern is identified as far as the degree of competition and the size of location planning is concerned.

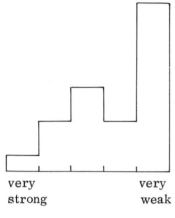

very strong   very weak

Extent to which competition was experienced on the product market during the location planning (Q 73)

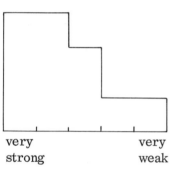

very strong   very weak

Extent to which competition on the labour market was experienced during the location planning (Q 74)

Extent to which competition was experienced on other resource markets during the location planning (Q 75)

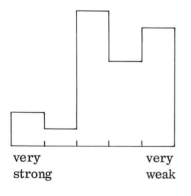

very strong   very weak

There are few variations regarding different periods of time. Looking at the three cases of failure (case number 12, 16 and 23), we find that one is related to a small "inflow of orders" but another (case no 16) is associated with very large demand. This data does not give support to the hypothesis that the perceived demand is related to either success or failure.

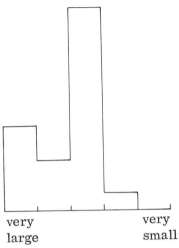

The relative demand perceived from the time of awareness until the time of the interview (Q 76)

very large

very small

To sum up this section: None of the proposed relationships, R 6 - R 20, received the required support. No additional hypothesis can therefore be formulated. But looking separately at each factor, interesting data has been found. These findings may be summarized as follows:

R 6   Cause for and steps taken before the location planning is probably the most critical factor. This includes the historical background preceding the location planning. The variability between the cases, however, is large.

R 7   Attitudes to secrecy dominate, although they do not affect the number of actors involved.

R 8   None of the company characteristics examined - number of employees, total turnover, ownership and goals - shows any clear variation with the number of actors.

R 9   There does not seem to be any correlation between the size of location project and number of actors.

R 10   "Conflicts" were difficult to identify.

None of the conflicts mentioned concerned disparity of views between actors about the choice between different sites.

R 11   The initiator of the location planning is usually an actor.

The actors also often constitute impetus forces while there are few answers to the question of status quo forces.

The last place visited is the place that was selected.

The total number of man-days for site search is not large considering the importance of the location problem indicated e.g. by the size of the new workforce.

R 12   Production managers and managing directors are predominantly involved in location planning.

The actors are managers and seldom planners.

The actors are technicians.

All the 68 actors are men.

R 13   In more than half the cases, no Government support was given for building and site.

R 14   The amount of negotiation contacts does not vary positively with the amount of subsidies received.

The negotiation contacts are relatively small in the cases involving investment funds.

R 15   The negotiations regarding investment funds are made by the managing director and the Minister of Finance.

R 16   There are very few identified conflicts between authorities.

R 18   There are big differences between various places in Sweden as far as new locations are concerned.

There are big differences between a place within the Development Area and a place outside.

There are very big differences between a place within a "big town area" and a place elsewhere.

There are few differences between a place in Norrland and a place elsewhere.

There are two points of view concerning the attitudes towards Svealand and Götaland. One is that there are big differences between a place in Svealand (or Götaland) and a place elsewhere and the other is that there are not.

There are no obvious differences between sites within counties or municipalities.

Concerning social responsibility and prevailing industrial tradition no pattern is identified.

Large places are not preferred although the potential labour supply is bigger.

The actors would definitively not locate a plant in an isolated place in order to be alone and therefore not to have to compete for labour.

Certain places are not avoided because the prevailing attitude there towards industry is negative.

R 19   The competition perceived during the location planning on the product market was very weak, on the labour market very strong, and on the other resource markets neither strong nor weak.

R 20   The relative demand perceived for products is neither large nor small from the time of awareness until the time of the interview.

The first part of the analysis of the data is now concluded. In this chapter the aim has been to focus on the variables, the hypotheses, the factors and the relationships – i.e. all components of the extended model from chapter 3. The next chapter contains a complementary viewpoint based on the individual cases.

And Pooh looked at the knocker and the notice below it, and he looked at the bell-rope and the notice below it, and the more he looked at the bell-rope, the more he felt that he had seen something like it, somewhere else, sometime before.
(Winnie-the-Pooh)

CHAPTER 6   COMPLEMENTARY CASE-ORIENTED ANALYSIS

In this chapter a second kind of analysis is used, which aims to group the 25 cases in homogeneous types. The analysis is based on all the data acquired during the course of this study. Ten types are presented which constitute the result of a mental process. Finally on the basis of the three most important components of the extended model, a further set of typical patterns in location choice situations are described.

6.1   Introduction to a Typology of Location Choice Situations

In chapter 5, two components - variables and/or factors - were tested against the data. While in that chapter only minor parts of the extended model were analyzed, the approach in this chapter is to test the whole model against the data. The analysis in chapter 5 was based on the answers to the questionnaire. In this chapter all kinds of data acquired during the course of study are utilized.

A major conclusion from the analysis in the last chapter was that, on the whole, the extended model constitutes a good language to provide a systematic framework within which to analyze location problems. In this chapter a complementary analysis is adopted. The aim is to find similarities in the 25 different location choice situations by grouping them in homogeneous types. A further argument behind this comple-

mentary analysis is that some of the relationships investigated
(H 1 - H 5 and R 6 - R 20) may receive additional support, if samples
only of the 25 cases - i.e. each type - are considered.

There appear to be two broad methods by which the 25 cases could be
sorted into types. First, through an explicit numerically based process in which mathematical and statistical techniques have been utilized;
one recent example being Asplund (1974). And secondly through an in-
tuitive mental process which takes place over a fairly long period of
time; an example being Mintzberg, Ransinghani and Théoret (1973).
The second method has been adopted. The process of this study is
characterized as follows:

1.   The most central part of the basic research question is: "... where
a relocation or a branch location should be made?", which will be interpreted as follows: What forces, combinations or series of forces influence the search for and final selection of a site? This second question
forms the criterion when components - variables and factors - of the
extended model are determined to characterize the individual group of
cases.

2.   All kinds of data constitute input to the mental process. As well as
the answers to the questionnaire, which form the bulk of the data, there
are also the six localization processes, the telephone-letter study when
identifying the cases, the answers to the questionnaire and all the knowledge acquired in informal talks before and after the interview.

3.   The principle used in selecting components from the extended model
is that there should be the smallest possible variation within the types
and the largest possible variation between them.

4.   All classifications of the components finally selected to describe
the types below are supported by data from the data list (answers to
the questionnaire).

The chosen approach can now be summarized. The purpose is to classi-
fy location choice situations and thereby create a location choice typology.
A typology consists of classes or types of location choice situations and
constitutes one kind of result from an empirical investigation. The
theoretical structure which is a basis for classification of location problems is the extended model, which may be referred to as a taxonomy.
A typology is thus a specific number of types that have been identified
on the basis of a classification which in its turn is based on a taxonomy.
Cases that show similarities are brought together in one class. Ten
types will be presented. No significance should be attached either to
the order in which the types occur or to the proportion of cases in which

each type occurs. It is accepted that a different sample of cases would produce a different order and proportion.

In most studies there are considerably less than ten types. The unusually large number in this study is a result of the wide variations between the different cases.

The order of the types is based on the number of cases within each type, as shown below:

Name of the type		Case number
I	"Political bargaining"	8 9 15 18 21
II	"Snapshot"	1 2 7 10
III	"Heavy investment"	11 13 16
IV	"The inexperienced entrepreneur"	14 19 20
V	"The professional entrepreneur"	4 6 25
VI	"The independent branch"	17 22
VII	"Authority backing"	3 23
VIII	"Careless planning"	12
IX	"Public professional locator"	24
X	"Cooperation and openness"	5

6.2 Ten Types

The ten types will be presented in the form of short essay-like case histories. These will be linked to the extended model through a figure illustrating the relevant components - variables and factors - of each type. On the final page of the section, in one table, all relevant variables and factors of each type are indicated with crosses.

153

I "Political bargaining"

This type is basically a financial problem (cause for and steps taken before the location planning) and is characterized by a large number of other decision variables, often still undecided. The reason for this is that a plant location is initiated by the authorities (primarily the Ministry of Finance) through a process of political bargaining, in which the underlying motive of the company is an overall expansion. Big companies with investment

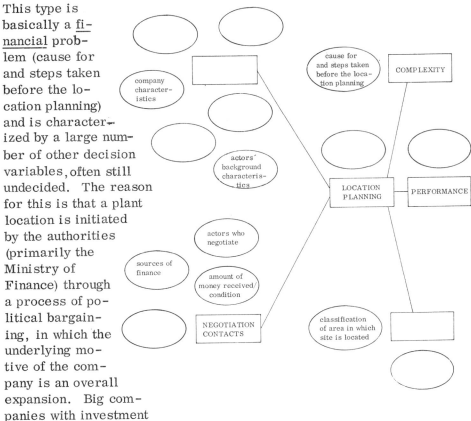

funds plan to use these when financing large investment programmes covering five years and amounting to several millions of Skr. The Ministry of Finance generally demands that the company locate a branch in accordance with the regional policy (COMPLEXITY) as a condition for allowing use of the investment fund.

The procedures characterizing the careful preparation of long-range investment plans are routine problems for the big companies included in this type of process (company characteristics). However, the costs for site searches are extremely low (LOCATION PLANNING). The insights concerning location problems and other kinds of unstructured problem-solving are large and the personal, emotional influence of the actors on the outcome of the location planning process is limited (actors' background characteristics).

Bargaining with the authorities is exclusively conducted between the managing director and the Minister of Finance and their contacts are very brief - a couple of hours only (actors who negotiate, NEGOTIATION

154

CONTACTS). The Minister himself or somebody near him suggests a place for the branch location. In two of the cases a specific place seems to have been proposed, while in the remaining three smaller areas with some possible alternative sites were mentioned. The company undertakes to employ a specific amount of labour. From my own investigation it would seem that companies are willing to accept any proposition from the Government. One possible reason for this might be time pressure. Possibly the start of the total investment programme could not be delayed (sources of finance). Companies seem to wait until the Ministry of Finance has specified its requirements before deciding what type of production to locate. Thereafter the location of the branch leads to a restructuring of the existing production system in which several plants are usually involved (amount of money received/condition).

The proposed alternatives for site selection are all within the Development Areas (classification of area in which site is located).

No failures were observed in the case of these big companies. There was no difference in the performance between expected and actual unit cost and planned expectations were met (PERFORMANCE).

II   "Snapshot"

This location choice situation is basically characterized as a capacity problem (cause for and steps taken before the location planning), i.e. in the case of large companies a combination of a substantial order with shortage of labour in the main plant which constituted the critical factor (company characteristics). The driving force is to acquire capacity quickly either at

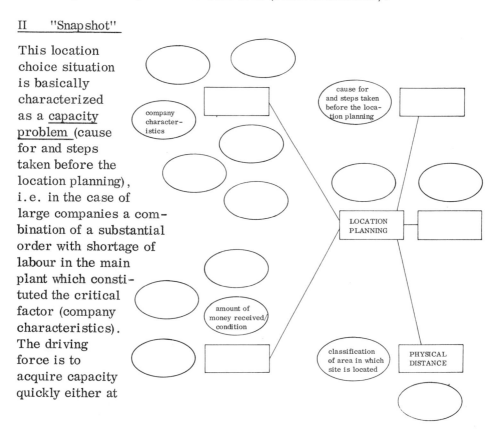

155

the main plant or on a new site nearby. A fully equipped plant without the delays of construction work and preferably with some key workers attached to it form the requirements. At some point somebody suddenly becomes aware of an empty building not far from the main plant. The search preceding this snapshot decision is passive in the sense that no sites have been visited. The decision procedure is also unsystematic and the number of data sources few. In three of the cases an actor became aware of the opportunity by reading advertisements in a daily newspaper and in the fourth case a solicitor from Ackordscentralen phoned and asked if the company was interested in taking over a firm that was going to be liquidated (LOCATION PLANNING).

There are no contacts to negotiate for subsidies (amount of money received/condition).

Since the purpose is simply to manufacture and provide the main plant with specific items, it is in no case considered necessary to involve senior management. The site is therefore selected very near the main plant so that it can be more easily controlled, and also to minimize the transport costs (PHYSICAL DISTANCE). It is necessary to find a site as close as possible, but where the local labour market is less "overheated". This means that none of these plants are within the Development Area (classification of area in which site is located).

III   "Heavy investment"

These locations are basically perceived as investment problems (cause for and steps taken before the location planning). They also occur in large companies, are prepared long in advance, and are regarded in the same manner as large single investments in heavy equipment (company characteristics). The question

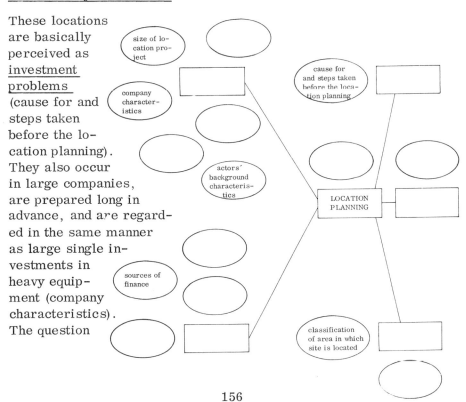

is often to decide whether to make the investment or not, i.e. to produce the particular goods or buy them from somebody else. The basic motives or driving forces behind the initiation of the location planning process are generally run-down localities and an uneconomical production process in combination with shortage of labour. The ground conditions of the sites are very carefully investigated and the results of the rigorous investment calculation indicate whether the investment is profitable or not. Any regional differences affecting profitability are not considered. The location planning is rigorous with a systematic decision-making procedure and a comprehensive data base (LOCATION PLANNING).

The financial side is not unimportant for the company since the plants are very large, labour intensive and expensive (size of location project). The search efforts are invariably directed towards the Development Area. Since the products are heavy however, an attempt is made to minimize the transport distance. The three cases of this type are all located in the very southern part of the Development Area. The Ministry of Finance is involved from an early stage of the planning, with the result that the company is assured of receiving financial help. In two of the cases the investment funds were released and in the third case a large location loan was granted (sources of finance).

There exist elaborate routines for investment planning and the actors' insights are generally wide (actors' background characteristics).

Negotiation contacts are principally with the owner of the site and, occasionally, with the local authority. They concern physical characteristics such as soil conditions etc.

The Development Area is chosen for financial reasons and because the actors think the supply of labour is sufficient in this area (classification of area in which site is selected).

IV   "The inexperienced entrepreneur"

This is a <u>launch</u> <u>problem</u> (cause for and steps taken before the location planning). A particular product forms the central aspect of the business idea and also the starting-point of this process. One person, an entrepreneur, has an idea which he intends to develop. The basic motive is highly personal and favours factors involving risk-taking. "To do something extra in one's life, to launch" (company characteristics).

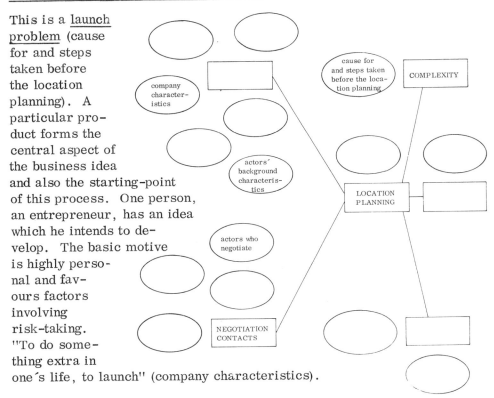

Uncertainty is very great since this is the entrepreneur's first location and therefore many other decision problems are unsolved (COMPLEXITY). Support from the local authority is of great significance, a fact which governs the search for sites; the financial problems are of critical importance. When these are solved, i.e. when the application for grants and/or loans is supported, the other decisions will be taken immediately.

The situation is very ill-structured and non-routinized for the entrepreneur who does all the location planning himself. His insights are small since he has no experience of location problems (actors' background characteristics) and therefore in the three cases which fall into this category, the number of sites visited and the outlays for the search were very large (LOCATION PLANNING).

Grants and/or loans from the National Labour Market Board (Arbetsmarknadsstyrelsen, AMS) are a necessity for starting up the plant. To secure these a number of contacts are made with civil servants at the middle and lower levels. This official procedure takes a very long time (NEGOTIATION CONTACTS).

158

The Development Area is selected because the entrepreneurs (actors who negotiate) apply for different kinds of subsidies (not site and building) from the Government subsidy scheme.

V   "The professional entrepreneur"

This is another capacity problem (cause for and steps taken before the location planning) and the type is also characterized by an initial product. However in this case the entrepreneur has met with the situation before. He has started up at least one company before, although he has not necessarily selected a location site (actors´ background characteristics). In these cases this individual,

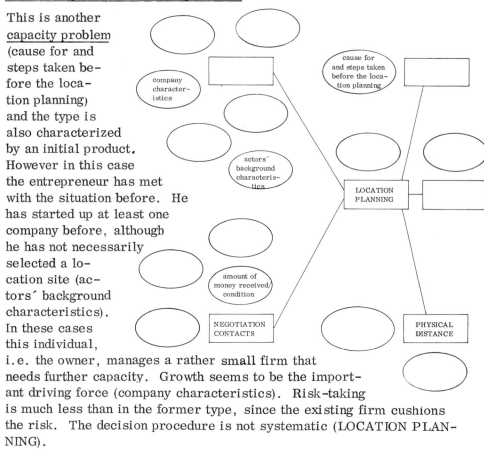

i.e. the owner, manages a rather small firm that needs further capacity. Growth seems to be the important driving force (company characteristics). Risk-taking is much less than in the former type, since the existing firm cushions the risk. The decision procedure is not systematic (LOCATION PLANNING).

No negotiation contacts are made since the finance problem is already solved (NEGOTIATION CONTACTS, amount of money received/condition). Support from the local authority is not required.

The sites selected are very close to the existing plant (PHYSICAL DISTANCE).

VI   "The independent branch"

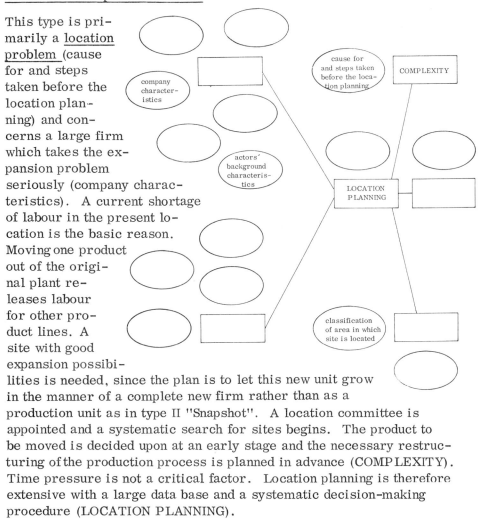

This type is primarily a <u>location problem</u> (cause for and steps taken before the location planning) and concerns a large firm which takes the expansion problem seriously (company characteristics). A current shortage of labour in the present location is the basic reason. Moving one product out of the original plant releases labour for other product lines. A site with good expansion possibilities is needed, since the plan is to let this new unit grow in the manner of a complete new firm rather than as a production unit as in type II "Snapshot". A location committee is appointed and a systematic search for sites begins. The product to be moved is decided upon at an early stage and the necessary restructuring of the production process is planned in advance (COMPLEXITY). Time pressure is not a critical factor. Location planning is therefore extensive with a large data base and a systematic decision-making procedure (LOCATION PLANNING).

Personal influences on the process are small. Though insights gained from other similar processes are extensive, the time and cost devoted to this type of planning process is fairly large (actors' background characteristics).

The plans are openly discussed with local authority representatives.

The motive is to find a site that meets the explicitly described requirements.

The supply of labour is regarded as being most promising within the Development Area (classification of area in which site is located). Larger towns are preferred since the purpose is to recruit people with higher education.

In this type <u>no problem is initially perceived by the company</u> (cause for and steps taken before the location planning). The initiative is taken by an active authority representative. A successful medium sized firm which does not have immediate plans for location is contacted by a national or local government civil servant. The authority promises support, grants or other subsidies, if the entrepreneur starts up a production unit in a specific place selected by the authority. The driving forces are the same as those in the types concerning small companies mentioned earlier, namely expansion and the expectation of higher profits.

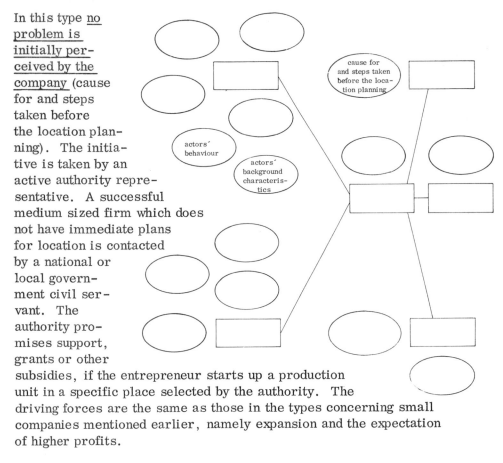

In the two cases covered by this type, the entrepreneur has experience from earlier location processes (actors´ background characteristics). However the only causal factor when determining the site is the suggestion made by the authority (actors´ behaviour).

The authority concerned – in the relevant cases the National Labour Market Board (Arbetsmarknadsstyrelsen, AMS) and a single local authority – arranges all financial questions and backs the company so that no real bargaining takes place. The selected area is wholly dictated by the authority.

The remaining three types are each based on one case only.

VIII "Careless planning"

In this type there is <u>no genuine business idea</u> (cause for and steps taken before the location planning) and the process is characterized by carelessness. The driving forces are unclear but seem to be based on some vague ideas about acquiring subcontracting jobs. A small firm from another Nordic country with one entrepreneur establishes a small plant managed by an employee

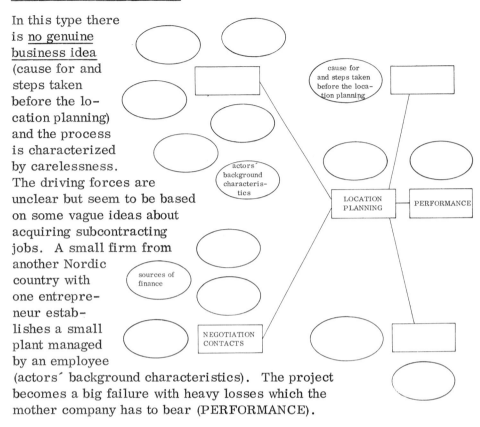

(actors´ background characteristics). The project becomes a big failure with heavy losses which the mother company has to bear (PERFORMANCE).

The process is non-routinized, since this is the first attempt to establish another plant. The employee conducts this job partly supervised by the entrepreneur. Location planning is very limited: few data sources, unsystematic decision-making procedure and a small amount of money spent (LOCATION PLANNING).

No contacts are made with any authority and no support is applied for, since the entrepreneur decides to choose potential sites outside the Development Area (sources of finance, NEGOTIATION CONTACTS).

IX   "Public professional locator"

The basic <u>problem</u>
in this type is
to <u>create job</u>
<u>opportunities</u>
(cause for and
steps taken
before the lo-
cation planning).
An authority, or
more precisely a
state-owned company,
intends to find new or existing business ideas and exploit
them (company characteristics). The exploitation is
planned to take
place within
the Develop-
ment Area
(classification
of area in
which site is
located).

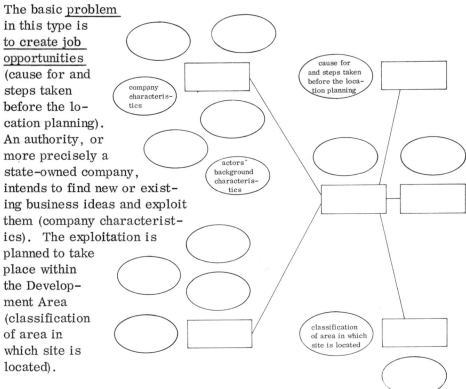

The insights about location planning and the knowledge
about sites within the relevant area are considerable. However,
the personal values of the professional locator are obviously a major
influence when it comes to choosing between different places (actors´
background characteristics).

The financial side of the project does not represent any uncertainty
since the "public professional locator" has informal contacts with
authorities granting subsidies and can easily get immediate answers.

X   "Cooperation and openness"

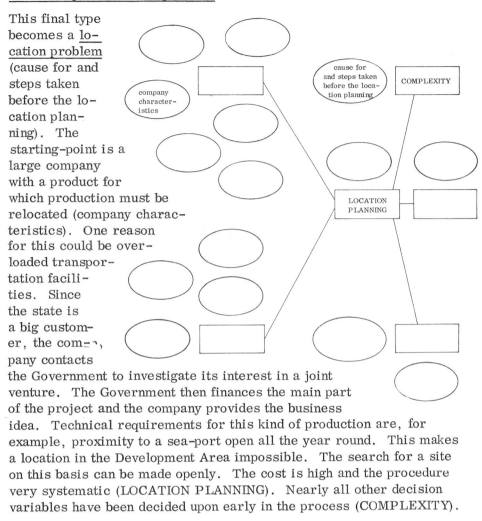

This final type becomes a <u>location problem</u> (cause for and steps taken before the location planning). The starting-point is a large company with a product for which production must be relocated (company characteristics). One reason for this could be over-loaded transportation facili-ties. Since the state is a big custom-er, the com₌₁, pany contacts the Government to investigate its interest in a joint venture. The Government then finances the main part of the project and the company provides the business idea. Technical requirements for this kind of production are, for example, proximity to a sea-port open all the year round. This makes a location in the Development Area impossible. The search for a site on this basis can be made openly. The cost is high and the procedure very systematic (LOCATION PLANNING). Nearly all other decision variables have been decided upon early in the process (COMPLEXITY).

The personal influence of the site searcher when evaluating different alternatives is rather limited. The criteria for selection must be de-scribed openly. However there is some indication that the final site selection is made by the Government.

The kind of contacts in this project are local authorities which make attempts to persuade top politicians in the Government and in Parlia-ment to influence the site selection in favour of their municipality.

164

A summarized description of all relevant variables and factors exhibited by each type is given in the following table.

Variables/factors	Political bargaining I	Snapshot II	Heavy investment III	The inexperienced entrepreneur IV	The professional entrepreneur V	The independent branch VI	Authority backing VII	Careless planning VIII	Public professional locator IX	Cooperation and openness X
Cause for and steps taken before the location planning	X	X	X	X	X	X	X	X	X	X
COMPLEXITY	X			X		X				X
actor´s attitude towards secrecy										
company characteristics	X	X	X	X	X	X			X	X
size of location project			X							
conflicts between actors										
actors´ behaviour							X			
actors´ background characteristics	X		X	X	X	X	X	X	X	
NUMBER OF ACTORS										
sources of finance	X		X					X		
amount of money received/condition	X	X			X					
actors who negotiate	X			X						
conflicts between authorities										
NEGOTIATION CONTACTS	X			X	X			X		
classification of area in which site is located	X	X	X			X			X	
attitudes to different areas										
PHYSICAL DISTANCE		X			X					
LOCATION PLANNING	X	X	X	X	X	X		X		X
competition										
PERFORMANCE	X							X		
demand										

6.3 Some Critical Forces in the Location Choice Situation

In this final section three of the most frequently utilized components of the extended model will be considered more fully. These are the factors "cause for and steps taken before the location planning" and "actors' background characteristics" and the variable "location planning". These components occur most frequently in the final table of section 6.2 and can be regarded as the most critical forces in the location choice situation.

"Cause for and steps taken before the location planning" is the most often used factor. This factor is the only one that refers to the period of time before t_1 i.e. before the start of the location planning. This factor covers the historical background of the perceived location problem. Past events and circumstances appear to have an extremely important bearing on any attempt to describe and explain a company's behaviour in location choice situations. Two aspects of this factor have been most frequently mentioned in the type descriptions: "What is the real basic problem?" and "Who is the basic initiator?" With regard to the first aspect, there were only a limited number of cases in which the actual search for the site was considered of prime importance within the company. Such cases occurred in the types "The independent branch" and "Cooperation and openness". In other types it was of secondary importance. For example "Political bargaining" principally involved a financial problem, "Snapshot" a capacity problem and so on. Secondly, concerning the initiator, in the type "Authority backing" the company is approached by an authority which heavily influences the site selection process. In all other types the location problem originates inside the company. When we consider the degree of outside influence on the site selection it is clear that authorities of various kinds play a major role. In "Political bargaining", "Heavy investment", "Cooperation and openness" and "Public professional locator" there seems to be a great deal of involvement.

The second component "actors' background characteristics" is frequently used in the type descriptions. Here the term "experience" often occurs, which indicates one important feature of location choice behaviour. That is, there are some types in which the actors have experience from similar location choice situations and others in which they do not. This conclusion is related to the conclusion that was drawn in chapter 5, namely that the actors are top management in a vast majority of cases. Surprisingly enough location planning is conducted by the top men, not only in small companies but in large ones as well. Each of the four conclusions below are based on evidence from the acquired data. They are not exclusive to any specific type but constitute important patterns which give a complete description of location choice behaviour.

1. The first reason why top management tackles this kind of problem
    is that it is not routine and no formal channels for dealing with it
    exist. Nobody in the organization feels any natural commitment
    to handle it.

2. Another reason for top management involvement is the character
    of the negotiation which location problems involve. One respondent
    said "The local authorities do not think the company is serious un-
    less the managing director pays a visit immediately". There seems
    to be a requirement that the representatives of the two sides in the
    bargaining process must belong to equivalent levels in their organi-
    zational pyramids. This conclusion is supported by several cases.

3. A third argument for top management involvement is the question
    of responsibility. Since the managing director is responsible for
    the result - the performance - after the start-up of the new plant,
    it is natural that he should also conduct the location planning.

4. Hence the manager continues to manage as he always has, receiving
    little help from the planner. But as organizations have become more
    complex, location problems have become increasingly concerned
    with such aspects as finance, product selection, capacity and so on.
    Changes in the characteristics of the manager's job - the growing
    fragmentation of skill, the increasing amount of verbal data with
    which he must cope, and the growth in the volume of decision-making
    in which he is involved - are assuming much more importance.
    Such characteristics in turn render the manager less able to cope
    with difficult problems and further reduce the planner's ability to
    help.

The third component to be further discussed is the variable "location
planning". The seven paragraphs below describe patterns of behaviour
which mainly lead to a reduced amount of location planning. These are
all based on evidence from at least one of the 25 cases.

1. It is difficult to decide whether new capacity should be provided
    within the existing plants or in a new place. After wasting a good
    deal of effort on this decision, the second step - where to locate -
    is given marginal attention. That is to say, limited location plan-
    ning takes place. Everybody is happy and relieved that a decision
    has been made and regards the whole problem as solved. This
    conclusion is particularly supported by the "Snapshot" type.

2. Planning is scanty because there are neither well established
    principles for good management, nor precise criteria for a good
    location site, nor principles leading to an ultimately successful
    performance. It is therefore very difficult to blame a decision-
    maker for lack of rigour in location planning.

3. Top managers are not used to identifying alternatives. This explains why so few location sites are visited. Usually alternatives in other problem areas are presented by subordinates and the managers only select. Top managers frankly do not know how to generate alternatives from scratch. Another conclusion is more plausible in some cases. Top managers know how to generate possible sites but the lack of time makes elaborate investigations impossible.

4. There is a view prevailing that the location problem basically is not an economic-business problem but a technical problem. The main reasons are either that the top management are technicians fashioned by their formal education or, more probably, that the approach is based on production-system thinking. This kind of thinking definitely dominates the two types "Heavy investment" and "Snapshot". For these reasons location planning, according to my definitions, will diminish.

5. A vast amount of prior knowledge exists: sophisticated models, frameworks and theories or intuition on the part of the actors. Such knowledge cannot be measured with my instruments. This could mean that what appears to be a small amount of location planning could in fact be a very elaborate kind of "intrinsic planning".

6. Actors tend to believe that location factors do no vary substantially from region to region. That is, that it does not really matter where the plant is located. This can in turn depend on the view that the future is impossible to predict, or that the adaptability of a plant is so large that some initial differences are of no importance in the long run. Such attitudes constitute explanations of some cases where limited location planning was observed.

7. The possibility of new employment opportunities make the company´s location problem an important matter for the public. Therefore the mass media in general and local newspapers in particular show a lot of interest in actors visiting new location sites. This seriously disturbs the search for sites, since it creates social pressure. By only examining a small amount of data and visiting a limited number of sites, the risk for discovery is diminished.

The analysis of the field research presented in this chapter and in chapter 5 is now completed. On a basis of these findings some implications for different categories of people will be discussed next in the final chapter.

But Owl went on and on, using longer and longer words, until
at last he came back to where he started ...
(Winnie-the-Pooh)

CHAPTER 7   CONCLUSIONS AND IMPLICATIONS

The preceding six chapters are briefly summarized below. This
summary is followed by some comments on validation and on the
generality of the current study. Some practical guidelines for
managers involved in location planning, obtained during the empirical investigation, are then presented. These are often based on
single observations and should thus not be regarded as generalizations. An alternative approach to regional planning, which might
be used to evaluate existing policy, is then suggested. Some
suggestions for future policy are also included. Finally, some
fruitful directions for future research are described.

7.1   Summary and Critical Review of this Study

This section consists of three parts. The first briefly describes the
six preceding chapters; the second discusses some methodological
issues concerning validation; and the third considers the degree of generality of the analysis and the results, bearing in mind the starting-
points described in chapter 1.

Since industrial location is usually associated with regional problems
and policy on a national level, chapter 1 presents the wider context in
which the company's decision-making occurs. One conclusion is that
the role played by government incentives and subsidies is not sufficient-

ly described in the literature, and that the efficiency of the instrument of government control would benefit from increased knowledge about the individual company´s behaviour when locating new plants. Despite some differences in regional problems between different countries, the nature of the location problem is the same in principle. The purpose of the study is to answer the basic question: How do companies behave in situations of location choice, i.e. when they face the problems of when, how and, primarily, where a relocation or a branch location should be made?

The problem of location, seen from both the government´s and the company´s point of view, has been studied from the perspective of a number of different disciplines. The frame of reference of this investigation is primarily based on theories of general decision-making and on theories and empirical observations of localization processes. The conclusions about the features of location selection situations which can be drawn from the latter type of literature are that the location decision is:

1. only one of the array of decisions that a firm has to make in location choice situations;

2. often low programmed or non-routinized, due to the lack of experience of location decision-making;

3. ill-structured, since neither the criteria for accepting a solution nor the data upon which it is based are particularly well defined, and

4. difficult to validate.

Answers to the basic question require empirical data and were sought by posing and answering five research questions. The manner in which these questions were approached was dictated by the discussion in the first chapter which demonstrated the importance of describing actual localization processes and the need for field observations.

In chapter 2 an answer was given to the research question: "What forces - variables and factors - affect the behaviour in location choice situations i.e. in localization processes?" Six case-studies, all of which were based on informal interviews, were investigated in order to identify major properties and forces affecting the behaviour of those involved in these situations. The research was carried out by studying existing documents, as well as conducting informal interviews. The interviews lasted between four and eight hours. The average number of respondents per firm was two, and in most cases these people can also be regarded as the key actors in the location planning process.

In chapter 3 six variables based on the localization processes of the previous chapter were identified. These variables are interrelated and suggest five hypotheses. The variables and the hypotheses constitute the basic model. The central variable is "location planning", which is defined as the number of sources used – i.e. the number of publications, models and techniques and people consulted – during the process which ends in a site selection.

Next the variable "complexity" was defined as the interrelation between the location decision and seven other major decisions identified in the cases. The degree of complexity is high when none – or only few – of the seven other decisions have been taken before the search for a site is started. The complexity is low when a majority of the seven other decisions have been made beforehand. The number of people involved in the process preceding the location decision was defined as the "number of actors". This constitutes the third variable. In order to acquire financial support from the authorities, the company applies for subsidies. The fourth variable "negotiation contacts" was defined as the number and duration in hours of contacts with the authorities for negotiation purposes. Fifth, "physical distance", was defined as the number of kilometres between the old and the new site. Finally the sixth variable, "performance", was defined as the extent to which the success or failure of the location is assessed by the person interviewed. The hypotheses below form five general conclusions from this first empirical study:

H 1 (hypothesis 1):   The degree of "complexity" is negatively related to the amount of "location planning".

H 2:   The "number of actors" is positively related to the amount of "location planning".

H 3:   The number of hours for "negotiation contacts" is negatively related to the amount of "location planning".

H 4:   The size of the "physical distance" is positively related to the amount of "location planning".

H 5:   The amount of "location planning" is positively related to the "performance" i.e. the greater the amount of location planning the higher the probability of success and, the smaller the amount of location planning the higher the probability of failure.

In the remainder of the chapter, the extended model was presented. This was constructed by posing and answering the questions: "What relevance have the variables which have been introduced?"; "What other methods of measuring these variables exist?"; "What factors influence the values of the variables?" The answers to these questions were primarily based on the case-studies, but a wide range of existing theories and empirical observations was also used. 15 factors were identified and it is argued that these factors affect the variables through 15 distinct relationships (R 6 - R 20). The research question dealt with in this chapter: "What are the general variables and factors and how are they related?" was answered through the extended model. The model, which is shown below, also provides the basis for a larger field study.

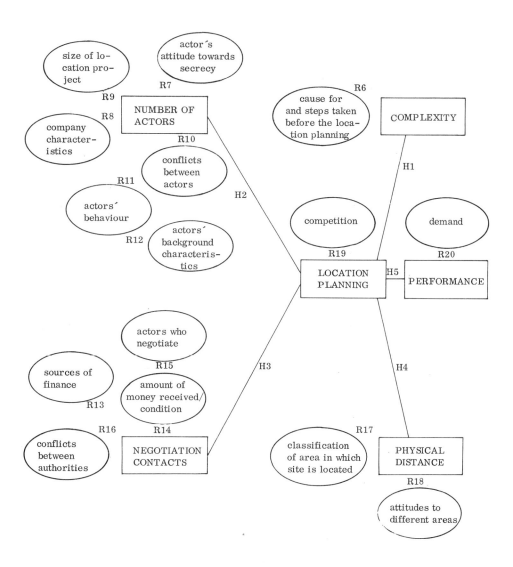

In chapter 4 the third of the five research questions was considered:
"How should a field study be designed to verify the generality of the
variables, factors and relationships?" After discussing different
methods the empirical field study was characterized as follows:

- interview

- analytical structured

- retrospective approach

- limited number of cases

The cases studied were selected from those location processes in the
engineering industry in Sweden with production start-up during 1970 –
1971 which satisfy the following criteria:

1. One year after start-up at least half the employees must have been
    recruited from the area around the location site.

2. The total number of employees at the new location one year after
    start-up had to be 25 or more.

These were identified by a combined telephone and mail approach to
three categories of administrative units in each county. The accuracy
of the information obtained in this manner varied considerably, which
suggested that it must be difficult for the Government to estimate the
effects of its regional policy. However, a total number of 48 cases
fulfilling the requirements were identified. These were contacted by
telephone, a preliminary investigation which reduced the number to 26.
Of these all but one were studied. A total of 49 respondents were interviewed, of whom a high proportion were from top management. The
interviews were based on a questionnaire which in turn was a formalization of the extended model.

The data thus acquired were presented in two complementary ways.

The first, in chapter 5, aimed at analyzing individual variables, factors
and paired relationships. This analysis was based on answers to the
questionnaire. The values and distributions of the six variables were
described. It should be borne in mind that two of these variables, "location planning" and "performance", were defined in more than one way.
In the subsequent statistical test only limited support for the relationships was obtained. The results were as follows:

- The degree of "complexity" was negatively correlated with the four attributes of "location planning". This supports hypothesis H 1. However, none of the correlations were statistically significant.

- The correlations between "number of actors" and "location planning" were insignificant and thus did not support hypothesis H 2, especially as the largest correlation coefficient was negative.

- The number of hours spent in "negotiation contacts" was positively correlated with all four attributes of "location planning". Thus H 3 should be rejected and replaced by the opposite hypothesis i.e. that the amount of negotiation is positively correlated with the amount of location planning.

- "Physical distance" was significantly correlated with one attribute of "location planning", but the correlations with the other three attributes were weak and insignificant. Thus hypothesis H 4 was only supported to a limited extent.

- Though one aspect of "performance" did vary significantly with three of the definitions of "location planning", taken generally the relationships between the four definitions of location planning and the six measurements of performance were too disparate to support hypothesis H 5.

The remaining components of the extended model i.e. the 15 suggested relationships were then analyzed by logical reasoning. A number of interesting conclusions were drawn, based on the description of the factors. The overall conclusion was that the differences in the cases as reflected in the data were too great for generalizations to appear. On the whole, however, it was concluded that the extended model constitutes an acceptable framework within which to analyze location problems.

In chapter 6 a complementary manner of analyzing the data was used. This was to group the 25 cases into homogeneous types. This analysis was based on all the data acquired during the field study, not merely the answers to the questionnaire. The cases were sorted into types intuitively over a fairly long period of time. The types were presented in the form of short essay - like case histories. They were linked to the extended model through a figure illustrating the relevant components - variables and factors - of each type. On the basis of the three most important components, a further set of typical patterns in location choice situations was described. These components are:

1. "cause for and steps taken before the location planning"

2. "actors´ background characteristics"

3. "location planning".

In the remainder of this section the validity and generality of the study will be discussed.

The term <u>validation</u> has earlier been used to characterize a localization process. This means predicting the success of the decision on the basis of the rigour of the procedure leading up to it. This specific meaning of the concept will be further discussed below. There are a number of definitions and classifications of the concept of validity. Unfortunately there is no generally accepted conceptual framework (Boalt, Erikson and Jonsson, 1971, p. 156, Nunnally, 1967, p. 99).

However, the statements below following Nunnally (1967, p. 75) summarize a common view of what validation is:

1. In a very general sense, a measuring instrument is valid if it does what it is intended to do.

2. Validation always requires empirical investigations, the nature of the evidence required depending on the type of validity. Validity is a matter of degree rather than an all-or-none property, and validation is an unending process.

It must be emphasized that only minor parts of this study aim at "measuring" in its traditional sense. This makes validation less relevant in this study. Assuming that the extended model is a "measuring instrument" and considering the basic question: "How do companies behave in situations of location choice, i.e. when they face the problems of when, how and, primarily, where a relocation or a branch location should be made?" it can be concluded that the extended model is a good language to analyze location problems. The "instrument" may therefore be regarded as valid since it does what it was intended to do.

In addition to this general view, three types of validity will be discussed: criteria validity, content validity and predictive validity.

<u>Criteria validity</u> means the degree of coincidence between simultaneous values of the same variable (Boalt, Erikson and Jonsson, 1971, p. 157). It is thus a measure of the consonance of different attributes (questions) of the same variable/factor. The variable "performance" has been shown to have rather high criteria validity, while the variable "location planning" presents a somewhat more heterogeneous picture. The re-

175

maining variables are only indicated by one attribute. Considering the other components of the model, namely the factors, it is impossible to estimate any criteria validity due to the scaling problem.

Content validity "depends primarily on the adequacy with which a specified domain of content is sampled" (Nunnally, 1967, p. 79). The major standards for ensuring content validity are 1) a representative collection of items, "questions", and; 2) "sensible" methods of test construction (ibid, p. 81). The selection and formulation of questions are thus crucial for content validity. Since no similar models with attached questionnaires from other studies are available, this method of validating is not possible here. There are, however, some circumstances which favour a relatively high content validity. The questionnaire was assessed from a methodological and design point of view at a number of seminars. It was also examined and revised by two people who had experience from recent location choice situations. Finally the respondents expressed the opinion during the interviews that the questions covered the vital aspects of location planning.

Predictive validity is relevant when the intention is to use an instrument to estimate some important form of behaviour. The term prediction refers to functional relations, e.g. correlation scores between an instrument and events occurring before, during, and after the instrument is applied. In most prediction problems, it is reasonable to expect only modest correlation. This conclusion is particularly relevant to location planning, which is generally low programmed and consequently must have a limited predictability. The analysis of the hypotheses (H 1 - H 5) resulted in conclusions that have some predictive value. There is still a long way to go before useful instruments can be constructed and used to predict the location planning procedures which will result in the selection of specific sites. The possibility of constructing instruments to predict the regional distribution of industrial activity is therefore even more remote! A limited contribution to the construction of such predictive instruments has been presented in the analysis above.

Finally, the generality of the results obtained in this study - a matter which is clearly linked to the concept of prediction - will be commented upon. This will be done from the viewpoint of the definitions and restrictions introduced in chapter 1.

1.   The retrospective approach means that only location problems and location processes that have led to a final decision are considered. From a methodological point of view the problems inherent in this approach are memory failure and retrospective rationalization. This always occurs in such studies. There is no evidence that these errors are systematic.

In addition it was discovered during the course of the field work
that localization processes in the companies had frequently been
started only to be interrupted for a variety of reasons. Despite
the lack of systematic evidence, it seems quite reasonable to apply
the extended model to such situations as well, despite the fact that
no final decision had been taken and no performance had appeared.

2. Though in many cases the location problem was dominated by other
    kinds of problems, e.g. investment problems or finance problems,
    the experience of this study is that there are large differences
    between "new-site" and "old-site" problems. No general conclu-
    sions will therefore be drawn outside the field of new-site locations.

3. Although the investigation was restricted at an early stage to the
    area of "footloose" (free to locate anywhere) industries, the evi-
    dence acquired suggests that parts of the analysis, particularly the
    extended model, are also applicable to companies in other types of
    industries with location problems.

4. The condition that the workforce must be "new" proved to be
    highly relevant. This factor distinguishes location problems from
    those of merger and takeover. The main points of this report
    consequently only apply to situations where the search is either
    for a "greenfield" site or for a site with a building but without an
    established workforce.

The remainder of this chapter is devoted to implications. Based on
analyses and results from this study, a number of consequences for
three different categories of people - managers, regional policy makers
and researchers - are suggested. These implications are related to the
systems levels introduced earlier in the following manner. The implications for the manager relate primarily to the "location management
system", but secondarily also to the "company system". Those for the
regional policy makers relate to the "environment system".

7.2 Implications for the Manager

There is a vast amount of literature (operations research models,
handbooks, guidelines etc) outlining the necessary steps to take, before
making a final location decision. The approach of this study is somewhat different, namely to offer advice on how to avoid pitfalls during
location planning. It is not intended to present a complete normative
process. The variations between different location choice situations
are too great to make this relevant.

The statements below are views and advice which are all based on evidence from the acquired data, which is predominantly of an informal and confidential character. The suggestions are based on examples of faults, mistakes and pitfalls identified by managers in the companies studied and also by other people with experience of location problems. Some of the suggestions are supported by observations from only one company; other statements are based on two or more cases. But in the final analysis, the statements are based on my assessment of observed behaviour.

The statements are arranged under five headings: What kind of location? What effort should be devoted to location planning? How should the analysis proceed? Who should do the location planning? What kind of information is needed and where can it be obtained?

1. What kind of location?

    – Is it really necessary to move? What pros and cons are attached
      to a move? Keep the alternatives to expand on the existing site
      or locate a new plant open, and investigate them simultaneously.

    – Investigate why the location of a new plant was suggested for the
      first time. Elaborate location planning may be unnecessary since
      certain factors may make a particular location and procedure
      inevitable.

    – The location project may have to be carried through, although
      circumstances have changed and a new plant is no longer the
      optimum solution. One case revealed that projects on which a
      great deal of effort has been expanded tend to be carried through
      to completion. The background factors in such situations may be
      prestige and role expectations. The project can also have grown
      to such a magnitude that it has acquired a life of its own and no-
      body questions whether a location is necessary or not.

    – It is expensive to start up new establishments. Calculate the
      need for excess liquidity during the first 2-3 years. The Govern-
      ment has no subsidy schemes for start-up losses.

2. What effort should be devoted to location planning?

    – It is not uncommon for the company to devote immense effort to
      deciding whether to move or not. Once the decision to move has
      been taken, it is vital that the subsequent search for a site also
      receives adequate time and effort.

178

- The costs allocated to location planning are in many cases strikingly limited. More resources should be devoted to the search for sites. Certainly the value of planning is dependent on a number of factors, such as: 1) The possibility of planning at all (access to reliable data, access to knowledge about relationships between important factors, possibility of determining targets, norms and requirements); 2) the alternative value of planning resources, e.g. top management´s allocation of time between different activities; 3) the degree of freedom of choice, i.e. the sensitivity of the company to different geographical positions.

In spite of these factors it is very important to emphasize that the location decision is of a gravity requiring more effort from management, in terms of time and money, than was shown in the cases investigated in my study. This statement is primarily supported by the impact of a location on a company´s profit. The company being a social unit, it is also necessary for the management to take social and regional effects into account, such as job opportunities, vocational training, housing and transportation facilities.

3. How should the analysis proceed?

- The location decision is only one of an array of decisions. It is suggested that at the outset all necessary decisions should be identified. These should then be separated into those which have already been made, those which are self-evident and those which require further investigation.

- Larger companies, which are quite often involved in location problems, should establish a routine procedure for location planning. This might include a periodic evaluation of a company´s site, which could be done by a location audit (also proposed by Otterbeck, 1973). A continuous feedback of the performance after the start-up date is imperative.

- If investment funds are going to be used, the company must think of possible products which could be located in places suggested by the Ministry of Finance. If this work is done in advance, the time pressure is less, and the possibility of reaching advantageous negotiation conditions better.

4. Who should do the location planning?

- Since location problems are regarded as a special kind of production planning, economists and business planners should be involved in location planning. Top management forms a necessary part of the group which ought to be made responsible for the project.

   – Let the top management negotiate, but have other people available too with more time to perform the laborious tasks such as data collection.

5.   What kind of information is needed and where can it be obtained?

   – Since the life of a plant is generally long, the planning must be long-range.

   – It is better to acquire considerable amounts of good information about different places – even if local newspapers write misleading articles about it – than to act without information.

   – Public statistics in Sweden are comprehensive. Many of them can be used in location planning. (The statistics on located firms are, however, less reliable).

   – Labour market calculations are necessary. Examine the availability and the skill of labour in cooperation with the local employment office.

   – Investigate the possibility of getting financial grants/loans and other kinds of support from different authorities. The bigger the company, the easier it is to get an answer in advance.

   – The local authorities often offer cheap land, electricity, water and sewage installations, and as a rule fulfill these commitments. The location planning group should investigate all such facilities.

   – Try to get the local authority to reveal other firms´ location or expansion plans. The supply of labour can be much reduced if another plant within commuting distance is established simultaneously.

   – When acquiring information from local authorities and county representatives, remember that they are regionally based. The National Labour Market Board (Arbetsmarknadsstyrelsen, AMS) and governmental people are to a lesser degree locally oriented. They also have a better overall view and can suggest places where real unemployment exists.

7.3   Implications for Regional Policy Makers

Very early in this study a number of public reports dealing with the means and ends of regional policy in Sweden were listed. The most recent of these reports (SOU 1974:82) suggests a new government authority to coordinate all location activities and grant permission for the majority of all locations. This is a more restrictive instrument than the earlier means of government control, and its aim is to increase government influence on the individual company´s site selection. The principal purpose of such control activities is to reduce unemployment within different regions. Tighter government control makes the need for good instruments to evaluate the results of government actions even greater.

Looking at earlier assessments of regional policy the following indicators seem to have been frequently used:

1.   The sum of money spent on subsidy schemes. Such statistics are less reliable and, in addition, the amounts really disbursed have not been fully investigated.

2.   The number of located firms. These statistics are less reliable, as has previously been shown.

3.   The degree of regional unemployment. These statistics are good, although methods for measuring the labour supply in other dimensions than number and occupation are limited or nonexistent.

While all these approaches use public statistics, the alternative suggested here is based on the location planning of the firm.

On the basis of this, two "regional policy variables" will be postulated: Since full employment is the basic government goal, the first regional policy variable, which is called "size", is the creation of new jobs. It can be assumed that large companies (here defined as employing more than 400 people) generally create larger plants with more new jobs than do smaller firms. The second suggested regional policy variable is called "involvement". This is defined as the extent to which an authority representative influences the final site selection. It has been shown that the involvement of authorities (who can be supposed to represent the full employment goal and aim at steering the new locations to under-employed regions) differs in different kinds of location planning. The conclusion drawn from this is that in situations where existing involvement is great, the authorities should be less interested in direct government control than in cases where it it limited.

By dividing both the "size variable" and the "involvement variable" into two groups based on magnitude, it is possible to construct the matrix shown below. The ten types of location choice situations identified in chapter 6 can then be distributed amongst the squares, which will be referred to as "regional policy situations".

Size / Involvement	Large	Small
Considerable	"Political bargaining" "Heavy investment" "Cooperation and openness"	"Authority backing" "Public professional locator"
Minimal	"Snapshot" "The independent branch"	"The inexperienced entrepreneur" "The professional entrepreneur" "Careless planning"

To assess these "regional policy situations" the 25 cases investigated may be distributed amongst the squares. This gives a rough estimate of the influence of regional policy on site selection. For each square the total workforce employed in all the cases studied at the end of the first and second years was calculated. It is clear that the effect of regional policy is most marked in the two situations in which "involvement" is "considerable".

Size Involve- ment	Large	Small
Considerable	9 cases 1661 employees after one year 2326 employees after two years	3 cases 236 employees after one year 318 employees after two years
Minimal	6 cases 232 employees after one year 282 employees after two years	7 cases 250 employees after one year 427 employees after two years

On this basis regional policy makers would be advised to concentrate their efforts on situations where current involvement is "minimal" but the acting companies are "large": A variety of regional policy schemes would probably be most successful in this situation. Although "small" companies according to this study seem to be better off without authority "involvement", this is not true when the cases are studied separately. And it is obvious that from an employment point of view the efforts should start with the large companies.

The order in which the regional planners might concentrate their attention is shown as follows:

	Large	Small
Conside- rable	3	4
Mini- mal	1	2

7.4   Implications for the Researcher

This final section will be divided into two parts. The first considers
manners in which an empirical investigation could be conducted in the
light of the experience I have gathered during the study. The second
part presents some directions for future research.

The design of the total study is traditional from one point of view. There
are two steps: the first aiming at generating a set of hypotheses by examining six processes, followed by a second step of hypotheses tests
in which 25 location processes are investigated. This design proved to
be very fruitful when conducting the field research.

The first point concerns the manner of presenting the results from the
larger field study. This experience is positive i.e. traditional pair-
wise analyses of variables/factors complemented with a situation - specific analysis aiming at creating groups of homogeneous types are worth
recommending.

Secondly, the telephone proved to be an excellent and fast method of
gathering data. The questions must, however, be few, easily understood and easily answered. It is usually difficult to persuade top
management in larger companies to agree to long interviews, whereas
on the telephone, they tend to keep on talking. Generally, this method
requires that an atmosphere of confidence is created by the researcher
by sending an introductory letter in advance, giving basic facts about
the purpose of the research.

Thirdly, it is not possible to validate models of which the extended
model is an example since there are no instruments which prove the
relevance or validity of an introduced variable or factor. In fact the
introduction of each of these in itself constitutes a hypothesis. Despite
the objections raised, the analyses indicate that in general, the extended
model is a good language with which to analyze location problems.

Concerning possible improvements, the following components of the extended model should be considered. The variable "number of actors"
received limited correlation support in the test of hypotheses. There
were also occasional disagreements amongst those involved in location
planning. My advice is to interview all the people proposed by any
respondent. Though the suggested "performance" variable is important
when describing effects after a move, more consideration must be devoted to the "adaptive" behaviour adopted immediately after a location
is carried through. Some factors in the extended model received little
evidence in the empirical investigation due to lack of answers. These
factors were "conflicts between actors" and "conflicts between authori-

ties". Such questions should be avoided. Another factor, "attitudes to different areas", seems important and much data was available. The precise explanatory power of the factor, however, is not easy to determine.

Three primary directions for future research will now be suggested:

First, it must be born in mind when assessing the empirical investigation that there is insufficient evidence to support the suggested relationships. The statistical results did not give much support to the hypotheses, and the other relationships proposed in the extended model received limited confirmation. No additional hypothesis could be formulated. The conclusion drawn for future research is that further study must be made of the forces - variables and factors - affecting behaviour in location choice situations. The focus might be on the description and refined definitions of individual forces before effort is devoted to studying the relationships between them.

One of the drawbacks of the selection of studied processes is that a final location decision must have been made. It has been shown that the historical background is most important, i.e. included in the factor "cause for and steps taken before the location planning", and this background often includes a number of location processes which have been started and for some reason interrupted before the final site selection. The understanding of company behaviour would probably be increased if these incomplete processes and the reasons for their failure were investigated more thoroughly. It should be possible to identify such processes through a simple survey letter to administrative authority units and/or local authorities and/or companies.

Another important direction for future research would be the study of real-time processes. Before proceeding with additional research based on the models presented in this study, the extent to which subsequent rationalization prevails should be examined. There is always a risk of this in retrospective approaches, in which the actors do not conceptualize some parts of the real situation. The next step therefore would be to take part in a localization process as an observer or as a participant-observer. The fact that such an approach might also increase the knowledge of the reasons behind an interruption of a localization process is in accordance with the suggestion made above.

REFERENCES

Aharoni, Y. , 1966, The foreign investment decision process.
Boston, Mass.: Harv. Univ.

Albinsson, G. , 1972, Företagens ramar - hur går det med handlings-
friheten? in Blandekonomi på villovägar. Stockholm: SNS, pp. 44-58.

Allport, G.W. , 1954, The historical background of modern social
psychology in Lindzey, G. , (ed.), Handbook of social psychology,
vol. 1, Theory and method. Reading, Mass.: Addison-Wesley,
pp. 43-45.

Ansoff, H.I. , et al. , 1971, Twenty years of acquisition behavior in
America. London: Cassel and Company Ltd.

Ansoff, H.I. , et al. , 1970, Does planning pay? The effects of planning
on success of acquisitions in American firms. Long Range Planning,
vol. 3, No. 2, pp. 2-7.

Applebaum, W. , 1965, Can store location be a science? Economic
Geography 41, pp. 234-237.

Asplund, G. , 1974, Osäkerhetsfaktorer i företaget och dess miljö, en
taxonomisk studie. Stockholm: EFI.

Back, R. , Dahlborg, H. and Otterbeck, L. , 1970, Lokalisering och
ekonomisk strukturutveckling. Stockholm: EFI.

Bateman, M. , Burtenshaw, D. and Hall, R. , 1971, Office staff on the
move. Research Paper No. 6, Location of Offices Bureau.

Boalt, G. , Erikson, R. and Jonsson, E. , 1971, Att undersöka beteende.
Stockholm: Natur och Kultur.

Borin, L. , 1967, Lokaliseringsbeslut inom detaljhandeln. Stockholm:
EFI.

Bower, J.L. , 1970, Managing the resource allocation process: A study
of corporate planning and investment. Boston, Mass.: Harv. Univ.

Brown, A. J. , 1972, The framework of regional economics in the
United Kingdom. Cambridge: Cambridge Univ. Press.

Burns, T. & Stalker, G.M. , 1961, The management of innovation.
London: Tavistock.

Cameron, G.C. & Clark, B.D. , 1966, Industrial movement and the
regional problem. Edinburgh: Oliver & Boyd.

Carrier, R.E. & Schriver, W.R., 1968, Location theory: An empirical model and selected findings. Land Economics, vol. 44:4.

Cohen, M.D., March, J.G. and Olsen, J.P., 1972, A garbage can model of organizational choice. Adm. Sci. Quart., vol. 17:1, pp. 1-25.

Cook, S.W. & Selltiz, C., 1964, A multiple indicator approach to attitude measurement. Psychological Bulletin, American Psychological Association, USA, vol. 62, pp. 36-55.

Cyert, R.M. & March, J.G., 1963, A behavioral theory of the firm. Englewood Cliffs: Prentice-Hall.

Cyert, R.M., Simon, H.A. and Trow, D.B., 1956, Observation of a business decision. The Journal of Business, vol. XXIX, No. 4.

Dikeman, N.J., Jr., 1962, A procedure for selecting industrial possibilities for a community. Oklahoma: Univ. of Oklahoma.

Dixon, W. & Massey, F., 1957, Introduction to statistical analysis. New York: McGraw-Hill.

Downs, A., 1971, Decision making in bureaucracy in Castles, F.G., Murray, D.J. and Potter, D.C. (eds.), Decisions, organizations and society. Harmondsworth: Penguin Books in association with The Open Univ. Press, pp. 66-85.

Ekman, B., 1967, Den reella organisationen och val av beslutsfaktorer vid rekrytering av nyckelpersonal till svenska dotterbolag i utlandet. Uppsala: Uppsala Univ., Företagsek. inst. (Mimeograph)

Eversley, D.E.C., 1965, Social and psychological factors in the determination of industrial location. Papers on regional development, supplement to Journal of Industrial Economics, ed. by Wilson, T. Oxford: Basil & Blackwell.

Fulton, M., Plant location - 1965. Harv. Bus. Rev., March-April 1955, pp. 40-50.

Fulton, M., New factors in plant location. Harv. Bus. Rev., May-June 1971, pp. 4-50.

Galbraith, J., 1973, Designing complex organizations. Reading, Mass.: Addison-Wesley.

Glaser, B.G. & Strauss, A.L., 1967, The discovery of grounded theory. Chicago: Aldine Publ. Co.

Green, P.E. & Carmone, F.J., 1970, Multidimensional scaling and related techniques in marketing analysis. Boston, Mass.: Allyn.

Greenhut, M. L. , 1956, Plant location in theory and in practice.
North Carolina: Chapel Hill.

Greenhut, M. L. , 1959, An empirical model and a survey: New plant
locations in Florida. The Review of Economics and Statistics,
vol. XLI, No. 1, pp. 433-438.

Greiner, L. E. , Patterns of organization change. Harv. Bus. Rev. ,
May-June 1967, pp. 119-130.

Gruber, W. & Vernon, R. , 1970, The technology factor in a world trade
matrix in Vernon, R. (ed.), The technology factor in international
trade. New York: Universities - National Bureau Conference series
No. 22.

Grundberg, L. , 1972, Beskattningen som medel i regionalpolitiken.
Ekonomiska utredningsrapporter Nr 2. Stockholm: Sveriges Industriförbund.

Guteland, G. , 1968, Regionala produktionsbetingelser i Sverige.
Stockholm: Stockholms Univ. , Nationalek. inst. (Mimeograph)

Hamilton, F. E. I. , 1968, Models of industrial location in Chorley, R.J.
& Haggett, P. , (eds.), Socio-economic models in geography.
London: Methuen & Co. , pp. 361-424.

Hoover, E. M. , 1948, The location of economic activity. New York:
McGraw-Hill.

Hunker, H. L. & Wright, A.J. , 1963, Factors of industrial location in
Ohio. Columbus, Ohio: The Ohio State Univ. (Research monograph
No. 119.)

Hägerstrand, T. , 1953, Innovationsförloppet ur korologisk synpunkt.
Lund: Lunds Univ. , Geografiska inst. , avhandl. nr 25.

Hörnell, E. , Vahlne, J-E. and Wiedersheim-Paul, F. , 1973, Export
och utlandsetableringar. Uppsala: Almqvist & Wiksell.

Isard, W. , 1956, Location and space-economy. New York: MIT.

Jobin, B. , 1973, Erfarenheter av lokalisering till stödområdet - en
intervjuundersökning 1972. Stockholm: Sveriges Industriförbund.
(Unpubl. report.)

Johansson, J. , 1966, Svenskt kvalitetsstål på utländska marknader.
Uppsala: Uppsala Univ. , Företagsek. inst. (Mimeograph)

Junnelius, C. , 1974, Investeringsprocessens utformning vid olika orga-
nisationsstrukturtyper. Helsingfors: Svenska Handelshögskolan,
Ekonomi och samhälle, nr 22.

Katona, G. & Morgan, J.N., 1952, The quantitative study of factors determining business decisions. Quarterly Journal of Economics, vol. LXVI, No. 1.

Kindleberger, C.P., 1962, Foreign trade and the national economy. London: Yale Univ. Press.

Krumme, G., 1969, Toward a geography of enterprise. Economic Geography, vol. 45:1, pp. 30–40.

Kruse, A., Lokaliseringsbetingelser i Halland. Rapport nr 2. Industriell miljö i Halland. Länsstyrelsen i Hallands län och nationalekonomiska institutionen i Lund, May 1972.

Kuehn, A. A. & Hamburger, M.J., 1962/63, A heuristic program for locating warehouses. Management Science, vol. 9, No. 4, pp. 643–666.

Larsson, S-O., Mål och medel i regionalpolitiken. Uppsala: Uppsala Univ., Nationalek. inst., Dec. 1970.

Lefeber, L., 1958, Allocation in space. Amsterdam: North-Holland Publ.

Levin, B., 1974, Definitioner och statistik över nyetableringar, flyttningar och filialutläggningar. Stockholm: Stockholms Univ., Företagsek. inst. (Mimeograph)

Lindbeck, A., 1972, Centralisering kontra decentralisering in Blandekonomi på villovägar. Stockholm: SNS, pp. 11–43.

Lindblom, C.E., 1959, The science of "muddling through". Public Adm. Rev., vol. 19, pp. 79–88. Washington: American Society for Public Administration.

Lloyd, P.E. & Dicken, P., 1972, Location in space: A theoretical approach to economic geography. New York: Harper & Row.

Loasby, B.J., 1967, Making locational policy work. Lloyds Bank Rev., No. 83, pp. 34–47.

Lorange, P., 1973, The planner's dual role – A survey of U.S. companies. Long Range Planning, vol. 6, No. 1, pp. 13–16.

Luttrell, W.F., 1962, Factory location and industrial movement, vol. I and II. London: National Institute of Economic and Social Research.

Lösch, A., 1954, The economics of location. New Haven: Yale Univ. Press.

MacCrimmon, K.R., 1970, Elements of decision making in Goldberg, W., (ed.), Behavioral approaches to modern management. Gothenburg: BAS.

March, J.G. & Simon, H.A., 1958, Organizations. New York: Wiley.

McCrone, G. , 1969, Regional policy in Britain. London: Allen & Unwin Ltd.

McMillan, T. E. , Jr. , 1965, Why manufacturers choose plant locations vs. determinants of plant locations. Land Economics, vol. 41, pp. 239-246.

Mintzberg, H. , Ransinghani, D. and Théoret, A. , 1973, The structure of "unstructured" decision processes. Montreal: McGill Univ. Faculty of Management. (Working paper.)

Mikaelsson, G. & Winberg, T. , 1974, Karaktäristika över några lokaliseringsföretag. Stockholm: Stockholms Univ. , Företagsek. inst. (Mimeograph)

Morgan, W. E. , 1967, Taxes and the location of industry. Series in Economics, No. 4. Boulder, Colorado: Univ. of Colorado Press.

Mueller, E. , Wilken, A. and Wood, M. , 1961, Location decisions and industrial mobility in Michigan. Ann Arbour, Mich.: The Univ. of Michigan.

Neuhoff, M. C. , 1956, Techniques of plant location. Studies in Business Policy, No. 61. New York: National Industrial Conference Board, Inc.

Newell, A. , 1969, Heuristic programming: Ill-structured problems in Aronofsky, J. , (ed.), Progress in operations research, vol. 3, pp. 361-414. New York: Wiley.

Newell, A. & Simon, H. A. , 1972, Human problem solving. New Jersey: Prentice-Hall.

Nieckels, L. & Söderquist, C. , 1970, Några modeller och lösningsmetoder till lokaliseringsproblem. Stockholm: Stockholms Univ. , Företagsek. inst. (Mimeograph)

Normann, R. , 1973, A personal quest for methodology. Stockholm: SIAR-19. 2nd ed. (Mimeograph)

Nunnally, J. C. , 1967, Psychometric theory. New York: McGraw-Hill.

Nygren, B. , 1972, Förundersökning av nyetableringar inom svensk industri 1963 - 1968. Stockholm: Sveriges Industriförbund.

Otterbeck, L. , 1973, Location and strategic planning. Stockholm: EFI.

Popper, K. R. , 1954, Degree of confirmation. British Journal for the Philosophy of Science, vol. 5, pp. 143-149.

Rees, J. , 1972, The industrial corporation and location decision analysis. Area, vol. 4, No. 3, pp. 199-205.

Revelle, C. , Marks, D. and Liebman, J.C. , 1970, An analysis of private and public sector location models. Management Science, vol. 16, No. 11, pp. 692-707.

Rhenman, E. , 1975, Organisationsproblem och långsiktsplanering. Stockholm: Bonniers. (SIAR-S-59.) (Engl. ed. 1973, Organization theory for long-range planning. London: Wiley. SIAR-18.)

Rockley, L.E. , 1973, Investment for profitability. London: Business Books Ltd.

Rondén, A. & von Schwerin, F. , 1974, Investeringsfonder i regional-politiken. Stockholm: Stockholms Univ. , Företagsek. inst. (Mimeograph)

Rydén, B. , 1971, Fusioner i svensk industri. En kartläggning och orsaks-analys av svenska industriföretags fusionsverksamhet, 1946 - 1950. Stockholm: Almqvist & Wiksell.

Sandkull, B. , 1970, Innovative behavior of organizations. The case of new products. Lund: Studentlitteratur. (SIAR-21.)

Serck-Hanssen, J. , 1970, Optimal patterns of location. Amsterdam: North-Holland Publ. Comp.

Simon, H.A. , 1945, Administrative behavior. New York: The Free Press.

Stafford, H.A. , 1969, An industrial location decision model. Proceedings of the Association of American Geographers, vol. 1, pp. 141-145.

Stevens, B.H. , Brackett, C.A. and Coughlin, C.A. , 1967, An investiga-tion of location factors influencing the economy of the Philadelphia region. RSRI, Discussion paper No. 12.

Söderman, S. , 1971, Beskrivning av några företags filialutläggningar - lokaliseringsprocessen ur beslutsteoretisk synvinkel. Stockholm: Stockholms Univ. , Företagsek. inst. , forskningsrapport nr 58.

Söderman, S. , Plant relocation - a case history. Oxford, June 1973. (Unpubl. seminar paper)

Thorngren, B. , 1972, Studier i lokalisering. Stockholm: EFI.

Townroe, P.M. , 1969, Locational choice and the individual firm. Regional Studies, vol. 3, pp. 15-24.

Townroe, P.M. , 1971, Industrial location decisions - a study in management behaviour. Centre for Urban and Regional Studies. Birmingham: Univ. of Birmingham.

Townroe, P.M. , 1972, Some behavioural considerations in the industrial location decision. Regional Studies, vol. 6, No. 3, pp. 261-272.

Törnqvist, G. , 1972, Kontaktbehov och resemöjligheter in Regioner att leva i. ERU. Stockholm: Publica, Liber Förlag.

Weber, A. , 1909, Über den Standort der Industrien. Tübingen.

Whitman, E. S. & Schmidt, W.J. , 1966, Plant relocation. New York: AMA.

Wibble, A. , 1973, Selektiv ekonomisk politik. Stockholm: EFI.

Åberg, Y. , Regional productivity differences in Swedish manufacturing. Booklet from IUI, No. 55, Reprint from Regional and Urban Economics, 1973:2.

AMS. Meddelanden från utredningsenheten 1973:20.

EFTA. Regional Policy in EFTA. Industrial Mobility, Geneva. September 1971.

SAPPHO, Project, 1971, A study of success and failure in innovation sponsored by the Science Research Council and carried out at the Science Policy Research Unit, University of Sussex, vol. I and II.

SOU 1951:6, Näringslivets lokalisering.

SOU 1963:49, Aktiv lokaliseringspolitik, bilaga I (G. Törnqvist, Studier i industrilokalisering).

SOU 1969:49, Lokaliserings- och regionalpolitik.

SOU 1970:29, Decentralisering av statlig verksamhet.

SOU 1974:82, Samverkan för regional utveckling.

United Nations, 1967, Criteria för location of industrial plants. Economic Commission for Europe. New York: United Nations Publ.

Clark, B.D.   75, 80
classification of area in which site is located   80, 103, 143, 154-156, 160, 163
clinical unstructured   87
Cohen, M.D.   8
company characteristics   71-72, 100, 138, 154-156, 158-160, 163-164
company system   65, 73-74, 83, 177
competition   68, 108, 147
complexity   56-
conflicts between actors   72, 101, 137-138, 184
conflicts between authorities   77-78, 103, 142-143, 184
content validity   175-176
Cook, S.W.   80, 81
cooperation and openness   153, 164-165, 184
correlation analysis   118, 127-130
cost definition   67-68, 108, 122
criteria validity   175-176
Coughlin, C.A.   9
Cyert, R.M.   8, 53, 55, 72

Dahlborg, H.   11
demand   83, 109, 148
Dicken, P.   10
Dikeman, N.J., Jr.   9
Dixon, W.   117
Downs, A.   70, 71

EFTA,   2, 4
Ekman, B.   79
engineering industry   89, 173
environment system   65, 83, 177
Erikson, R.   175
error   52, 114
Eversley, D.E.C.   80
extended model   83-

face test   118, 127, 130-132
fact-finding   85
field observation   16, 170
field study   16, 49, 84, 86
footloose   2, 14-15, 89, 177
Fulton, M.   9

Galbraith, J.   70
garbage can model   8
general decision-making theories   7-8
generality   16, 85, 169, 176-177
Glaser, B.G.   18
Green, P.E.   118
Greenhut, M.L.   6, 9
Greiner, L.E.   74
Gruber, W.   78, 79
Grundberg, L.   75
Guteland, G.   6

Hall, R.   4
Hamburger, M.J.   4
Hamilton, F.E.I.   10
heavy investment   153, 156-157, 165, 182
Hoover, E.M.   14
Hunker, H.L.   9
Hägerstrand, T.   79
Hörnell, E.   79

ill-structured   12, 17, 52, 54
impetus forces   72-73, 138, 149
independent branch   153, 160, 165, 182
inexperienced entrepreneur   153, 158-159, 165, 182
informal interview   18, 68, 87, 170
intrinsic planning   168
Isard, W.   6

Jobin, B.   5, 89
Johansson, J.   79
Jonsson, E.   175
Junnelius, C.   7

Katona, G.   9
Kindleberger, C.P.   79
Krumme, G.   10
Kruse, A.   9
Kuehn, A.A.   4

Larsson, S-O.   75
Lefeber, L.   6
Levin, B.   13, 91
Liebman, J.C.   6

participant-observer 86, 185
performance 56–
physical distance 56–
political bargaining 153–155, 165, 182
Popper, K.R. 55
predictive validity 175–176
process theories 5–7
professional entrepreneur 153, 159, 165, 182
public professional locator 153, 163, 165, 184

questionnaire 86, 112, 152

Ransinghani, D. 152
Rees, J. 10
regression analysis 118, 127, 132–133
relocation 13, 19, 34–35, 37
retail location 4
retrospective approach 15, 176, 185
Revelle, C. 6
Rhenman, E. 76
Rockley, L.E. 70
Rondén, A. 75
Rydén, B. 90

Sandkull, B. 64
SAPPHO 64
Schmidt, W.J. 10, 11
Schriver, W.R. 9
Selltiz, C. 80, 81
semi-objective criteria 82, 110
Serck-Hanssen, J. 6
Simon, H.A. 7–8, 10, 12, 68, 72
size of location project 72, 101, 137, 156
snapshot 153, 155–156, 165, 182
SOU 1951:6 2
SOU 1963:49 2, 9
SOU 1969:49 2
SOU 1970:29 4
SOU 1974:82 2, 4, 30, 75–76
source definition 66–67, 105–107, 121
sources of finance 75–77, 103, 154, 156, 162
Stafford, H.A. 10
Stalker, G.M. 70
status quo forces 73, 138, 149

Stevens, B.H. 9
Strauss, A.L. 18
subjective criteria 82, 110-111
systems theory 65
Söderman, S. 18
Söderquist, C. 6

taxonomy 152
Théoret, A. 152
Thorngren, B. 4
time definition 68, 108, 122
Townroe, P.M. 3, 5, 10-11, 67-68, 71, 79-80
Trow, D.B. 8
typology 151-152
Törnqvist, G. 5, 9

United Nations 14

Vahlne, J-E. 79
validation 169-170, 175
warehouse location 4
Weber, A. 6, 79
Vernon, R. 78-79
Whitman, E.S. 10-11
Wibble, A. 76
Wiedersheim-Paul, F. 79
Wilken, A. 9
Winberg, T. 97
von Schwerin, F. 75
Wood, M. 9
Wright, A.J. 9

Åberg, Y. 5